I0810446

LOST LINCOLN PARK MICHIGAN

LOST
LINCOLN PARK MICHIGAN

CRAIG E. HUTCHISON

THE History PRESS

Published by The History Press
An imprint of Arcadia Publishing
Charleston, SC
www.historypress.com

Copyright © 2025 by Craig E. Hutchison
All rights reserved

First published 2025

Manufactured in the United States

ISBN 9781467145800

Library of Congress Control Number: 2025943123

Notice: The information in this book is true and complete to the best of our knowledge. It is offered without guarantee on the part of the author or The History Press. The author and The History Press disclaim all liability in connection with the use of this book.

All rights reserved. No part of this book may be reproduced or transmitted in any form whatsoever without prior written permission from the publisher except in the case of brief quotations embodied in critical articles and reviews.

This publication is dedicated to everyone who has ever had any role in the establishment of the area known today as Lincoln Park. From the early Native Americans to the European pioneers to those residing in Lincoln Park in the twenty-first century, each has played a role in crafting this community and helping develop the area into what exists in the present and setting the table for what the future could be. This book is dedicated to you.

CONTENTS

ACKNOWLEDGEMENTS

This book would not exist without the enormous support I received from the Lincoln Park Historical Museum. Chief Curator Jeff Day and Assistant Curator Adrian Ace assisted me in maneuvering through the museum archives in order to obtain amazing images that work in concert with the text and help provide enlightening visuals. Both Jeff and Adrian were instrumental in pointing me in the direction of background material I needed in my research, and I cannot say enough about how important it was to be able to use them as a sounding board and to ask necessary questions. I will forever be in their debt, and I am proud of what we accomplished together.

I would also like to thank Leslie Lynch-Wilson, president of the Lincoln Park Preservation Alliance. Leslie was a huge help in the early stages as I was organizing my thoughts and assisted me in what direction might be best. Also, Leslie was part of putting together an earlier book on Lincoln Park, and that publication was a great resource to me.

Projects like this are rarely done in a vacuum. So, with that said, I want to say how much I appreciate my wife, Kim, and my daughters, Abigail and Lydia. They were very encouraging throughout the evolution of the manuscript but especially as I began to work intensely to get the text count to where it needed to be and as I worked on my least favorite part of writing a book: captions. Lastly, I thank God for lending me a few talents to be able to put something like this together. Placing history into a printed page form is truly a passion, and I feel very blessed to have been part of this project. I hope anyone who has ever been associated with Lincoln Park is honored by this effort.

INTRODUCTION

The story of Lincoln Park is a tale that incorporates numerous elements and a wide array of characters. It is a story of freedom but also of loss; of beauty and transformation; ingenuity and hard work; building and decline; hope and fulfillment. Hundreds of years ago, one must imagine a much less developed world. Before there were border lines drawn defining the city of Lincoln Park, the area was a vast forest of oak, hickory, ash and whitewood. A wide river was not far away, a body of water that would later be called the Detroit River. Two additional waterways flowed inland that would be much closer to the early inhabitants. The earliest people in the area were Native Americans known as the Wyandot and the Potawatomi. Between the water and the forest, this land was amazing grounds for hunting and fishing. Deer, bear, fox and other fur-bearing animals were plentiful and provided the area tribes not only with sustenance but also tools for their existence. Life remained this way for many centuries until the coming of people known as Europeans.

With the coming of the British specifically, it became clear that "a way of living" for the Native American tribes was changing, and the Odawa chieftain, Pontiac, was determined to do something about this change by plotting "the destruction of the encroaching white man." As the French and Indian War came to an end, Pontiac, along with other tribes living in the former French territory, did not find the British to be as peaceful as the French. In 1762, Pontiac sought support from Native tribes from Lake Superior to the lower Mississippi. His aim was to forge an alliance to help

Native peoples defend their land from encroaching colonists. In May 1763, Pontiac planned for every tribe to attack the British fort nearest to them and then to join forces and together attack colonial settlements.

Pontiac's plan was unveiled at what was the largest war council assembly of Native Americans in the Great Lakes region in history. The council took place in what is today the city of Lincoln Park. The Historical Society of Lincoln Park has erected a marker honoring Pontiac and chronicling the event at present-day Council Point Park.

Pontiac and his Odawa forces elected to capture Detroit. After his first assault failed, reinforcements came from the Wyandot, Ojibwe and Potawatomi. With this additional help, they started a siege that lasted months. On July 31, Pontiac won the Battle of Bloody Run; however, the British received reinforcements, and on October 30, Pontiac retreated to the Maumee River. The main plan was successful: eight out of the twelve forts attacked by the united tribes were captured. Most of the garrisons, several relief expeditions and settlements were wiped out.

In the spring of 1764, British troops were sent into Pennsylvania and Ohio and fought the Delaware and Shawnee until they signed a peace treaty, breaking Pontiac's alliance. With no support from the French or western tribes, Pontiac was forced to sign a treaty with the British in 1766. In 1776, leading chiefs of the Potawatomi Nation deeded a huge tract of land to a Frenchman living in Detroit; his name was Pierre St. Cosme. Most of present-day Lincoln Park is within the boundaries of that deeded land.

After the American Revolution, it became important to begin drawing boundaries. The Michigan Territory was officially created in 1805 by an act of Congress. The lure of inexpensive, quality land brought a slow influx of settlers from the east. But there was one huge impediment: the area was difficult to reach. The completion of the Erie Canal in 1825 brought with it a much less arduous journey. Early settlers could now ride up the Hudson River, through the Erie Canal to Buffalo, across Lake Erie by steamboat and up the Detroit River, which meets with the Ecorse River. The Erie Canal reduced what had been a five- to ten-day brutal land journey to a forty-four-hour water route.

Within the Northwest Territory and specifically, the Michigan Territory, an area known as Ecorse Township was created by an act of the Michigan legislature in 1827. This was ten years before Michigan was officially a state. The first Europeans to settle in the area were French. They built homes along the Detroit River and along the Rouge River and Ecorse Creek. The early families who made their way and settled here bore pioneer names that became well known, and many are still recognized today. Strip farms or ribbon farms were set up, which were only a few hundred yards wide on the riverfront but extended back into the forest for miles. This ensured access to a water source for the greatest number of people. Future generations built their homes farther back from the rivers. Some of the earliest homes built within the present borders of Lincoln Park were located along the southern edge near Goddard Road. An 1818 map of the area shows homes only in this section. Throughout most of the early 1800s, the area was largely dense forest broken only by the occasional farm clearing.

As the 1800s moved along, German immigrants purchased farms in the western section of Ecorse Township. As German settlers pushed east toward the Detroit River and French settlers moved inland, the two groups met and began to build a community.

After the Civil War, there were many thriving farms, and the beginnings of a business district sprang up at Fort Street and what was then known as the St. Cosme Line (later called State Street and today known as Southfield Road). Herman Quandt opened a grocery market at this crossing in 1899. Soon, other businesses opened nearby, and by the time World War I began, a community known as Quandt's Corners had been established. The building of the Ford Rouge Plant nearby and Henry Ford's offer of five dollars a day along with other industrial places of employment sparked rapid population growth for the area. Employees at Ford Motor Company were looking for housing, and the Lincoln Park area was in a prime position to fill that need. From the end of World War I through the 1920s, there was a huge real estate boom.

In 1921, a handful of residents met and approved plans for the incorporation of the Village of Lincoln Park. Many have questioned why the name Lincoln Park was chosen for the new entity; that topic will be covered later in this book. After many additional square miles had been annexed to the village and to provide protection from other communities encroaching on village land, it was proposed that the village be reincorporated as a city. In 1925, that proposal was placed before the population and approved. Lincoln Park would now be identified as a city.

Lincoln Park grew steadily over the next several decades. The reason for this is something every real estate agent espouses: location, location, location. The city was close enough to industry so that on one hand, the proximity meant a short commute to good-paying jobs. At the same time, Lincoln Park was far enough away from manufacturing complexes in order to not suffer from the pollution that normally accompanies industrial facilities. Accessibility and convenience cannot be overstated: Lincoln Park was only three miles from the Ford Rouge Plant, two miles from the Great Lakes Steel Corporation plant in Ecorse, three miles from manufacturing plants in Wyandotte and less than a ten-minute drive from hundreds of factories in Detroit. That was the view outward. Looking inward, those who guided the city in its early days had the foresight to push for infrastructure improvements such as access to adequate water, a sewer system, paved streets and quality schools.

The 1960 census shows that the population had risen, by that time, to 53,933. In 1960, the city ranked as the fourth largest in Wayne County behind only Detroit, Dearborn and Livonia. Through the twentieth century, the city earned the moniker "bedroom community" because while there was no industry within its borders; those who lived in Lincoln Park commuted to industrial jobs. During the 1950s, a second growth spurt occurred with the building of two major shopping hubs: Lincoln Park Plaza in 1955 and the Lincoln Park Shopping Center in 1956. The city continued to thrive over the next two decades. In less than half a century, Lincoln Park had been transformed from a densely forested area with narrow, muddy streets and little in the way of commercial development to a modern, attractive residential community with paved streets, healthy neighborhoods, shopping centers and decent schools.

An economic downturn in the 1970s and increasing competition in the greater area caused the business community to suffer a downturn at the dawn of the twenty-first century. Many businesses either closed or left. In 2014, the city was declared to be in a state of fiscal emergency, and an emergency manager was appointed. By 2017, Lincoln Park had made a remarkable comeback and wiped out its operating deficit and instead had built up a positive fund balance. Employment numbers have improved in the last decade. The prime real estate where the former Lincoln Park Shopping Center stood will soon be filled with business condos; shops, restaurants and retail will be on the first floor, with condos just above. Another sign of Lincoln Park's renaissance is the influx of Hispanic-owned businesses opening at a record pace in the downtown area. A great example of the past meeting the future can be seen in the transformation of the building that for over eighty years housed Chiarelli's Market (see chapter 7). Chiarelli's Market closed in 2008. The same structure is now being used by Los Arcos Market, which features a grocery store, meat market, carry-out and casual dining. When considering the history of the building, the present owner, Mario Briones, sees an interesting parallel that points to positive steps for the future of Lincoln Park: "What we do is the same kind of thing, but it's Mexican, and we serve food. We have a mixture of Hispanic clients and a lot who have lived here a long time who still call it old Chiarelli's."

Stories of structures like the one that has housed Chiarelli's and Los Arcos Markets are a powerful demonstration that the heart of Lincoln Park is still alive and well. The passion of the pioneers who built a community, the willingness to take a risk and be an integral part of a larger whole has not left the community and can be repeated. In these pages, the stories of those early builders are shared. What they did created a foundation for what was to come and is still something that the present and future generations can add onto. While many of the structures covered here—and indeed, a way of life—have disappeared, this history and these stories provide readers with something to be grateful for and to be inspired by in creating a better future. Nothing happens in a vacuum. In most cases, a foundation has to be laid by someone for others to come along later and add to it or at least use what has been built to transition into something else. Even mistakes that were made in the past must be absorbed in such a way so that they are not repeated. The aim of this publication is to hopefully provide readers with all of the above, which includes the steps forward, the steps back and many "eureka!" moments throughout the journey.

As this journey into the past begins, one word of caution. Not everything that has ever happened in the history of the Lincoln Park area is covered in this text. Not every building that was constructed and then torn down is discussed. Space limitations and availability of source material are huge determining factors in the research and writing of a publication like this. However, know this: every effort was expended to create, craft and produce a book that tells as many of the interesting stories related to Lincoln Park history and its structures as space permitted.

Chapter 1

EARLY HISTORY OF THE AREA

Long before Europeans arrived within the boundaries of what is referred to today as Lincoln Park, the land was prime hunting grounds of the Potawatomi and Wyandot tribes. While highways and neighborhood streets crisscross the entire area today, hundreds of years ago, the land was a vast forest of oak, walnut, ash and whitewood. The early residents hunted for various game, including deer, bear and fox. These animals provided sustenance and sought-after fur. Nearby branches of what would one day be named Ecorse Creek provided another channel of travel by canoe, and the water was full of life-giving pike, bass and trout.

The history of the larger area in terms of European settlement seriously began when Antoine de La Mothe Cadillac landed on July 24, 1701, near what is today Woodward and Jefferson Avenues in Detroit. The French had been in North America for almost one hundred years by that time spreading religion and establishing posts to facilitate fur trading. With further movement inland, a post was established at Fort Michilimackinac, where Cadillac served as commandant. Searching for a more suitable location for the control of the fur trade, he selected Detroit. Cadillac's entourage included one hundred French-Canadians and one hundred Algonquin Indians in twenty-five large canoes. Searching out the best possible site for a fortified town, Cadillac noticed that the narrowest part of the river was faced on each side by a bluff about forty feet high. With an eye for what would make the site more easily defensible, he chose the western side, where the bluff ended abruptly in a small hill. The party landed, climbed the bluff and claimed the land in the name of King Louis XIV.

Tribes gathered from hundreds of miles away on April 27, 1763, to meet at the confluence of the three forks of the Ecorse River (in present-day Lincoln Park) to discuss Chief Pontiac's plan to deal with the British. *From* Pontiac's War, *2007.*

By the mid-1700s, European powers Britain and France were vying for control of the Great Lakes region. In 1763, with the conclusion of the French and Indian War, the Great Lakes region officially came under the control of England. Many of the Native American tribes of the area were unhappy about this change, as they worried about their way of life being negatively impacted. Pontiac, a powerful and influential Odawa chief, was determined to stop the encroachment of the British.

In 1762, Pontiac sent emissaries around the region and as far west as the Mississippi River in order to gain support in challenging the British. Pontiac's plan was to attack the nine forts in the Ohio country and Great Lakes region at roughly the same time. He thought this plan would prevent the individual forts from supporting one another. Once the forts were captured, the tribes were to attack settlers in the various areas and kill as many as possible. These actions, Pontiac reasoned, would discourage future settlement in the area.

In the spring of 1763, Native warriors began making their way to the various British forts. But first, there was to be one last grand council meeting before the plan was put into motion. That meeting took place at the three forks of the Ecorse River, at a spot today known as Lincoln Park. It was one of the most far-reaching Native American councils in history, as numerous

Chief Pontiac presented a plan that called for attacks on British forts in the Great Lakes and Ohio Valley region. The attack on nearby Fort Detroit would be led by Pontiac. *From* Pontiac: Indian General and Statesman, *1974*.

tribes gathered from hundreds of miles away. The tribes included the six nations: the Odawa, the Huron, the Shawnee, the Potawatomie, the Ojibway and the Outagamies. It was their plan to reclaim their own lands. Pontiac, a charismatic leader, made passionate speeches that stirred the tribes who had assembled. After three days of council and war dances, Pontiac once again went over the details of his plan and assigned forts to each tribe.

Frank Rathbun, a reporter for the Mellus Newspapers and local historian, relates the following about the location of the council meeting:

> *History does not tell the exact location of the great assembly which drew warriors and chiefs from every tribe and nation of Indians in the Great Lakes region. We know only that it was held on the banks of the Ecorse River. Tradition relates, however, that it was at the confluence of the north and south branches of the Ecorse River, near the neck of land which still bears the name "Council Point" or Pontiac Point. The tepees of the huge band of warriors were probably erected throughout what is now Lincoln Park. The Historical Society of Lincoln Park erected a marker honoring Pontiac in Council Point Park.*

Pontiac's personal assignment was to capture Fort Detroit. His plan was to take the fort by surprise so that the lives of his men would not be endangered. Pontiac was unaware that the commander of Fort Detroit had been warned that an attack was coming. (Ironically, this warning came from the daughter of a French resident who was friendly with Pontiac.) Fort Detroit held out, and after a 153-day siege, reinforcements forced Pontiac to end the attack. Eventually, he saw no alternative but to smoke the peace pipe and accept the reality that the British would remain in the region.

While the exact location of the war council has been lost to history, the dedication of Council Point Park was documented. Rathbun, intimately familiar with the history of the area, was at the dedication of the park on September 16, 1956, and presented an informational and passionate speech about why the area has such historical significance:

> *Not many persons are aware that we, here in Lincoln Park, have a historic spot that ranks among the most important in Michigan in terms of historical significance.*
>
> *Two hundred years ago, a large group of Indians assembled on a spot only a few hundred yards from here, and planned what became the Indians' greatest attempt to keep the white man from taking over their hunting grounds.*

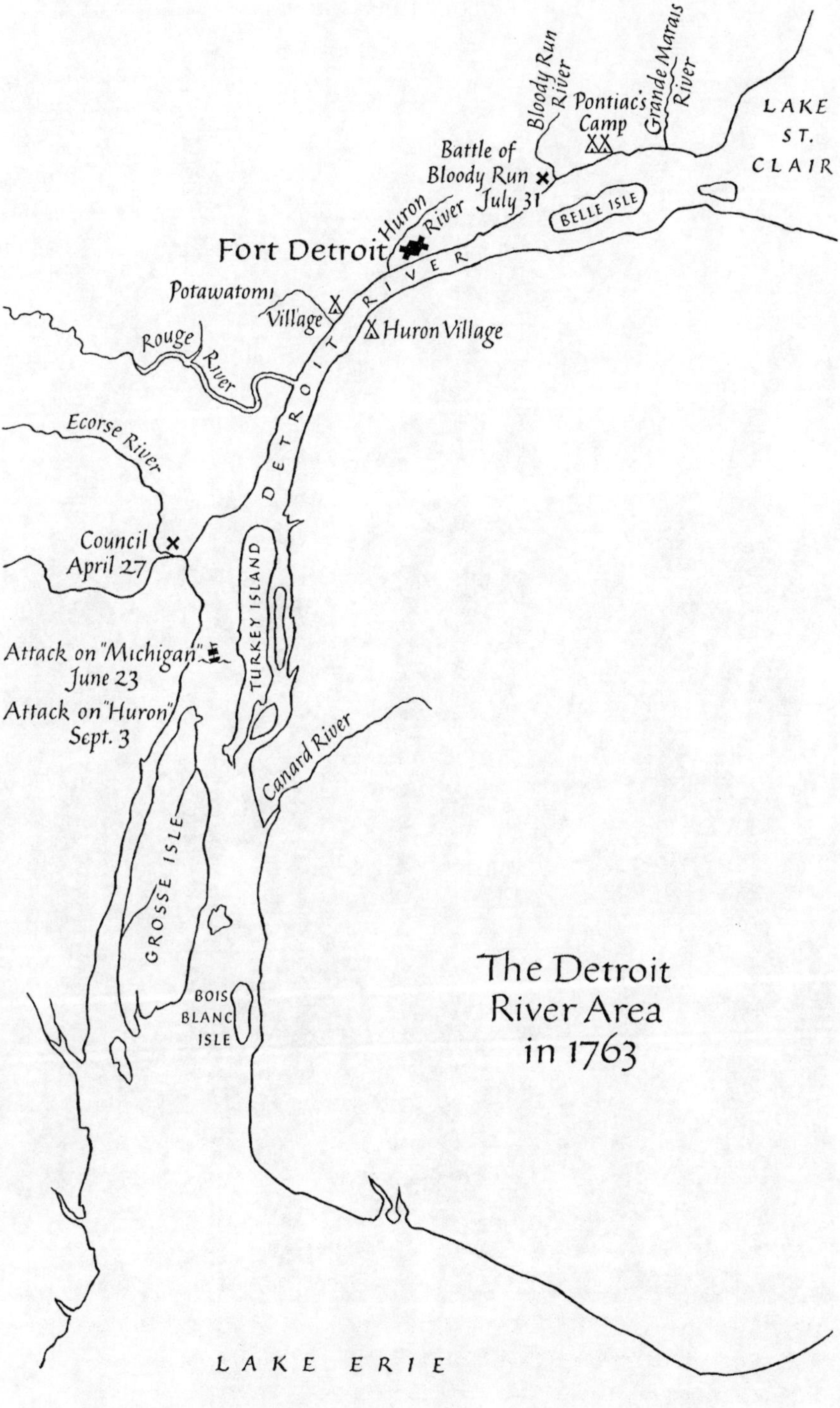

The site and the time for the intertribal war council, marked as "Council" on this map, was chosen by Pontiac, the Odawa chief. He chose a hidden location near Fort Detroit in what is today Lincoln Park. *From* Pontiac's War, *2007*.

In 1956, the Historical Society of Lincoln Park erected a marker and a rock honoring Pontiac in the first version of Council Point Park located at River Drive at the foot of LeBlanc Street. *Lincoln Park Historical Museum.*

The leader of this far-reaching project was the great Ottawa Chief, Pontiac, whose home was on Peche Island, near Belle Isle, in the Detroit River. Pontiac, then about 50 years, was the acknowledged leader over most Indian tribes of the Algonquin Stock in the southeastern part of Michigan. He was one of their bravest leaders in war, and one of their wisest counselors in peace; when he spoke, other Chiefs listened.

In 1760, after the English had defeated the French in what we know as the French and Indian War, all the forts in the Great Lakes region were turned over to the English by the French. Most important of these forts was at Detroit, near Pontiac's home. There is a legend—never really verified—that Pontiac went to the English Commander and asked that he, as a mighty Indian Chief, be made a general in the English Army. When his request was turned down, so the story goes, he resolved to gain revenge for what he considered a grievous insult.

Whatever his reason, Pontiac bitterly hated the British, and he conceived the idea of uniting all the Indians in the northwest into one confederacy to drive the Red Coats out of the territory. Pontiac received one big disappointment. The Powerful Iroquois Confederacy—the Six Nations of New York State—did not respond to his call. Only the Senecas came to his Council. The other five nations remained loyal to the English.

No record exists, of course, of Pontiac's talk. We can imagine, however, what he said. He reminded his listeners of their glorious past, when the entire continent was theirs alone. He reminded them of how the French had been the Indians' friends, and how the English had insulted them, took their furs in exchange for cheap whiskey, and refused to treat them as equals. He told them that the combined power of the Indian tribes could easily dislodge the English and make the land again the sole possession of the Indians. He told them that their great God Manito would be with them in battle, and he told them that the great French king would send help.

The assembled chiefs and warriors, seated around the Council fire, roared their approval of Pontiac's plan. The Shawnees were to strike at Maumee and Sandusky; the Winnebagoes at Green Bay, the Chippewas, Massasaugas and Outagamies at Michilimackinac, the Pottawatomies at St. Joseph, and the Senecas at Niagara and Fort Pitt.

Pontiac and his allies were to attack the important post at Detroit, which controlled the entrance to the Upper Great Lakes area. The Indians dispersed to their homes and prepared to put the scheme into operation. Pontiac first resorted to trickery to take Detroit. He and some 60 warriors went to the Fort, supposedly on a friendly visit but with sawed up muskets, knives and tomahawks hidden under their cloaks. Major Gladwin, the English Commander, was to be approached by Pontiac while the Chief was holding a wampum belt, white on one side and green on the other. If he gave the belt to Gladwin with the green side up, it meant that the attack should commence. Gladwin had been warned, however, and had his entire garrison standing by with ready muskets. Pontiac saw that his plot had been foiled, so he presented the belt white side up and he took his men away. They then began a siege of the Fort which was to last for five months.

Pontiac became more and more enraged, as reports came to him that the other Chiefs were succeeding. Michilimackinac fell, its garrison wiped out. Green Bay was taken. So was Maumee, St. Joseph, Sandusky, and other lesser Forts. Within a month, nine British posts were captured by the Indians. Only Detroit, Niagara and Fort Pitt held out. In the fall, reinforcements and supplies reached Detroit, and Pontiac and his allies grew tired of the struggle and abandoned the siege.

Although his grand scheme had failed, Pontiac's conspiracy left its mark on the northwestern frontier. An estimated 2000 settlers were killed in a huge area ranging from northern Wisconsin to northern Virginia. The situation became so bad that the English government forbade all new settlement beyond the Allegheny Mountains.

Pontiac's huge attack was well-planned, well-coordinated, and well carried out. It came close to succeeding. But the development of the American Continent was not to be stopped. Pontiac smoked the Peace Pipe with the English in 1765. And a few years later he was dead, killed by a Peoria Indian who reportedly had been bribed with a jug of whiskey by an English trader. Pontiac's murder stirred a furor among the Indians of the northwest, and thousands of Peoria Indians were killed in revenge.

In closing, I would like to read a few lines of a poet's interpretation of Pontiac's words here at Pontiac Point:

Hang the Peace Pipe on the wall, Rouse the nations one and all
Tell them quickly to prepare, for the bloody rites of war
Now begin the fatal dance, raise the club and shake the lance
Now prepare the bow and dart, Tis our fathers' ancient art
Let each heart be strong and bold, as our fathers were of old
Warriors UP, PREPARE, ATTACK, Tis the voice of Pontiac.

In 1999, a Community Development Block Grant sponsored a second dedication of Council Point Park, which included moving the rock from the original location and the historical signage that can still be viewed today. The text from the State of Michigan signage is reprinted below, and the site can be found at 3075 River Drive in Lincoln Park.

> [Front] *Council Point*
> *On April 27, 1763, Obwandiyag, an Odawa who was also called Pontiac, assembled a council of warriors from various tribes near this site. He urged them to fight to maintain control of their land and their way of life. For more than a century, tribes in the Ohio Valley and the Great Lakes had allied themselves with different European nations that fought to dominate the Great Lakes. Most favored the French, trading partners who were not very numerous, instead of the British, whose policies and exploding population were a threat to Indian existence. After the French lost the Seven Years' War (1756–1763), the tribes faced a single European power: Britain and its colonies. Their resistance began almost immediately with attacks on posts and forts.*
>
> [Back] *Pontiac's Council*
> *The Native American council that met near this site on April 27, 1763, included members of the Odawa, Potawatomi, Wyandot, Huron and Ojibwa bands. Pontiac told of Delaware prophet Neolin's vision of resisting the British and returning to traditional ways. The resulting plan to surprise and seize Fort Detroit on May 7, 1763, became a siege lasting nearly six months and involving more than 900 Great Lakes warriors. That summer thirteen other British posts were attacked. At Detroit, on July 31, the British attempt to engage the Indians failed disastrously at Bloody Run. In October, the French declined to provide support, and warriors returned home to their families. The siege ended, but the tribes' fight for their homelands and their rights continued.*

In April 2013, Lincoln Park had the unique opportunity to commemorate the 250th anniversary of Chief Pontiac's War Council held along the Ecorse River on April 27, 1763. This event, coordinated by the American Indian Movement's Michigan Chapter (AIM-Mi) and the Lincoln Park Historical Museum with support from the City of Lincoln Park, was held at Council Point Park.

In 1999, the marker and rock were relocated to the second Council Point Park at River Drive and New York Street. *Lincoln Park Historical Museum.*

The mayor of Lincoln Park at the time, Pat Krause, welcomed everyone and introduced presentations made by State Senator Hoon-Yung Hopgood and Wayne County Commissioner Ilona Varga. Grand Chief Ted Roll of the Wyandot of Anderdon Nation spoke of the Wyandot alliance with Pontiac.

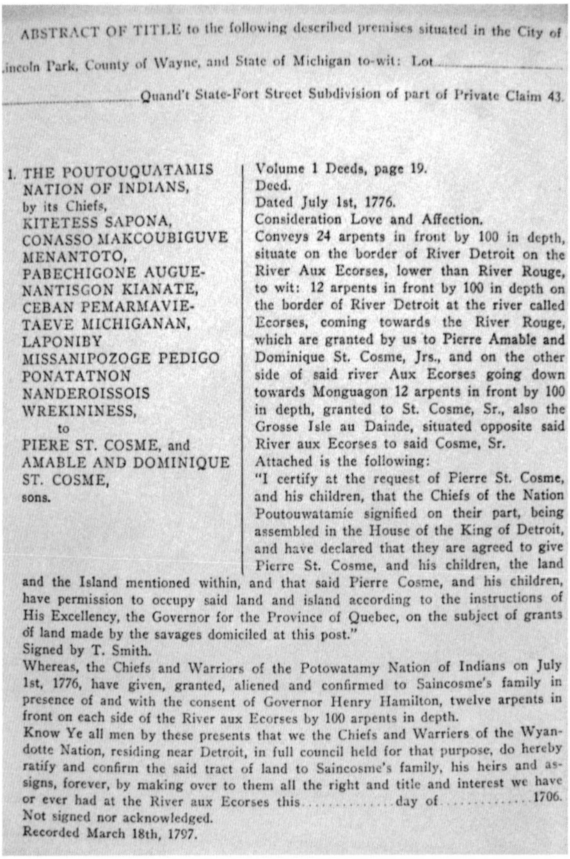

ABSTRACT OF TITLE to the following described premises situated in the City of Lincoln Park, County of Wayne, and State of Michigan to-wit: Lot ________________
________________ Quand't State-Fort Street Subdivision of part of Private Claim 43.

1. THE POUTOUQUATAMIS NATION OF INDIANS, by its Chiefs, KITETESS SAPONA, CONASSO MAKCOUBIGUVE MENANTOTO, PABECHIGONE AUGUE-NANTISGON KIANATE, CEBAN PEMARMAVIE-TAEVE MICHIGANAN, LAPONIBY MISSANIPOZOGE PEDIGO PONATATNON NANDEROISSOIS WREKININESS, to PIERE ST. COSME, and AMABLE AND DOMINIQUE ST. COSME, sons.

Volume 1 Deeds, page 19.
Deed.
Dated July 1st, 1776.
Consideration Love and Affection.
Conveys 24 arpents in front by 100 in depth, situate on the border of River Detroit on the River Aux Ecorses, lower than River Rouge, to wit: 12 arpents in front by 100 in depth on the border of River Detroit at the river called Ecorses, coming towards the River Rouge, which are granted by us to Pierre Amable and Dominique St. Cosme, Jrs., and on the other side of said river Aux Ecorses going down towards Monguagon 12 arpents in front by 100 in depth, granted to St. Cosme, Sr., also the Grosse Isle au Daiude, situated opposite said River aux Ecorses to said Cosme, Sr.
Attached is the following:
"I certify at the request of Pierre St. Cosme, and his children, that the Chiefs of the Nation Poutouwatamie signified on their part, being assembled in the House of the King of Detroit, and have declared that they are agreed to give Pierre St. Cosme, and his children, the land and the Island mentioned within, and that said Pierre Cosme, and his children, have permission to occupy said land and island according to the instructions of His Excellency, the Governor for the Province of Quebec, on the subject of grants of land made by the savages domiciled at this post."
Signed by T. Smith.
Whereas, the Chiefs and Warriors of the Potowatamy Nation of Indians on July 1st, 1776, have given, granted, aliened and confirmed to Saincosme's family in presence of and with the consent of Governor Henry Hamilton, twelve arpents in front on each side of the River aux Ecorses by 100 arpents in depth.
Know Ye all men by these presents that we the Chiefs and Warriers of the Wyandotte Nation, residing near Detroit, in full council held for that purpose, do hereby ratify and confirm the said tract of land to Saincosme's family, his heirs and assigns, forever, by making over to them all the right and title and interest we have or ever had at the River aux Ecorses this............day of............1706.
Not signed nor acknowledged.
Recorded March 18th, 1797.

Left: Pierre St. Cosme was granted a large tract of land by the Potawatomi Nation in 1776. The land grant included all of present-day Lincoln Park. *Lincoln Park Historical Museum.*

Opposite: The Northwest Territory was the first organized territory created by the Northwest Ordinance in 1787. The Northwest Territory included what is now Indiana, Illinois, Michigan, Ohio, Wisconsin and the northeast part of Minnesota. *Lincoln Park Historical Museum.*

Sharing the unique aspect of the French community at Detroit in 1763 was Ken Navarre, president of the Wyandotte Historical Society and a descendant of Robert Navarre, the official notary at Fort Detroit during the time of the Pontiac siege. Following the dedication, the "Seventh Generation" family of Chief Pontiac, members of the Saginaw Chippewa Nation and led by family member Ben Hinmon, held the Eagle Staff ceremony. The family unveiled the grand staff dedicated in honor of their great-grandfather Pontiac for this 250th anniversary occasion. Family members sang the Honor Song as part of the ceremony.

Only thirteen years after Pontiac's conspiracy failed, leading chiefs of the Potawatomi Nation deeded a large tract of land to a Frenchman living in Detroit. The Frenchman's name was Pierre St. Cosme, and on July 1, 1776, he and his two sons became owners of a piece of property that included most of present-day Ecorse, Lincoln Park, Allen Park and Wyandotte.

This huge land mass was granted to St. Cosme, according to the deed, for "love and affection." The date on the document was four days before the Declaration of Independence was adopted. After the completion of the American Revolution, ownership of the Great Lakes region passed from England to the United States, although the United States was unable to enforce its claim until 1796. The land became part of the Northwest Territory in 1787, the same year that St. Cosme died, and his family sold the land to farmers moving into the area. The names of the families who purchased the land would become well known in the Lincoln Park area: the Campaus, Salliottes, Labadies, LeBlancs, Goodells, Bondies and Drouillards.

The early farms these pioneer settlers established became known as "strip farms" or "ribbon farms," as they fronted either the Detroit River, the Rouge River or the Ecorse River and ended on the edge of the St. Cosme property, a border that became known as the St. Cosme line. As homes were built farther back from the rivers in later years, the first homes were built in what would eventually be called Lincoln Park. A log house built by Hubert Champagne in 1845 is a prime example of the type of construction that was used in the time of the pioneers. Hubert was born in Frenchtown (Monroe), and the first Champagnes were listed in the 1750 census as early Detroit-area settlers. The log house originally stood on what would become Champagne Road, named for these pioneers. To make way for Champagne Road, the house was moved to White Street just west of Dix Avenue. In 1975, the structure was torn down, and a new house was constructed on the lot.

Many of the early log cabins were built with hand-hewn logs. Some of the logs measure more than a foot thick. The logs were notched at the ends to fit together. The spaces between the logs were filled with a mixture of clay, moss, hay, stones or wood. This process was called "chinking" or "daubing." The inside walls were covered in plaster or whitewash. Most floors were beaten earth, but some cabins had floors of puncheons. Fireplaces were built at one end of the cabin with a hearth made of stone or clay. Most log cabins were a single room, about twelve to sixteen feet square. They had one door and usually no windows. If windows were cut into the walls, animal skins or

This log cabin was built by Hubert Champagne in 1845 and is a prime example of the type of construction that was used at the time. The log cabin originally stood on what would become Champaign Road. *Lincoln Park Historical Museum.*

The Peter Drouillard home was near Goddard Road and Fort Street. Peter Drouillard, a descendant of a pioneer family, is second from the left. *Lincoln Park Historical Museum.*

boards were used to cover the openings. Most log cabin roofs were steeply pitched and the rafters usually covered with wooden shingles. Over the life of the cabin, wood siding would often be placed over the hand-hewn logs for preservation.

In the first half of the 1800s, the area was largely a dense forest. As waves of pioneer families settled in the area, the clearing of the forests happened at a faster rate. In time, the area was growing not only in terms of settlers and log houses they built, but one could also see the beginning of a business district and what could be described as a small downtown area.

One of the families connected to the ribbon farms was the Drouillard family. Emigrating from France to Canada in the eighteenth century, the family eventually made its way to Montreal, then to a suburb of Windsor and eventually crossed the Detroit River to Detroit. In 1808, Jean Baptiste Drouillard purchased land from the St. Cosme family. The land ran between the Detroit River and the Ecorse River in what would eventually be called Lincoln Park. Toussaint Drouillard, son of Jean Baptiste, bought a ribbon farm near Goddard Road and Fort Street. Peter Drouillard was the grandson of Toussaint and lived his entire life on the family farm located at 1130 Goddard Road.

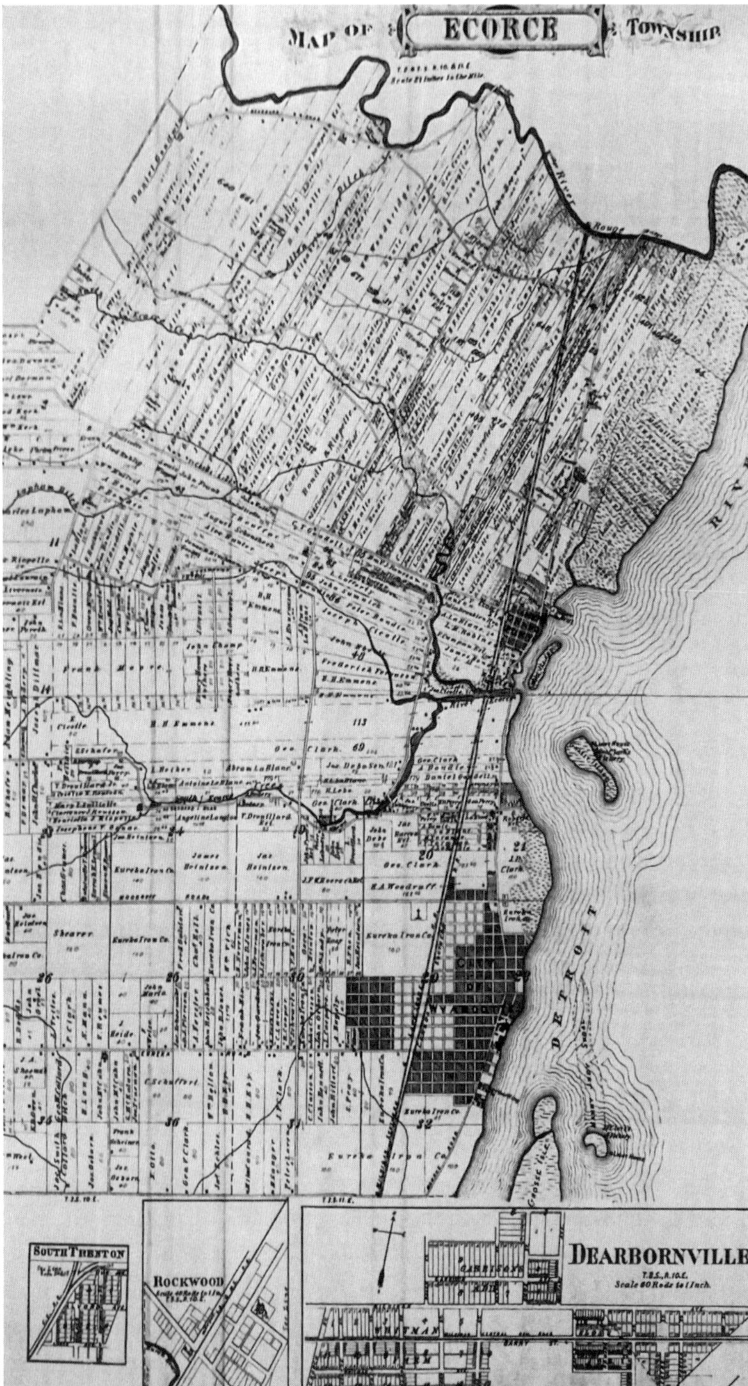
MAP OF ECORCE TOWNSHIP
SOUTH TRENTON
ROCKWOOD
DEARBORNVILLE
DETROIT

During the presidential term of John Quincy Adams between 1825 and 1829, Congress divided the Michigan Territory into townships. In 1827, Ecorse Township was formed, but years before that, a small fishing and farming center had sprung up along the Detroit River. In 1836, Simon Rousseau, A. Labadie, L. Bourassa and P. LeBlanc made the first plat of a village and officially named it Grandport. At that point in its history, the village of Grandport had eight hundred people, 152 homes and four businesses. It became the hub of the neighboring sprawling farmlands and the site of a shipyard as well as Raupp's Lumber Mill.

Early maps show the village of Grandport and the streets named on the map still exist in present-day Ecorse, some showing the same names they did over a century and a half ago. Streets in the village of Grandport were named for historical figures, including Andrew Jackson, Daniel Webster and James Monroe. Webster and Monroe Streets still exist in Ecorse today. High, Labadie, Bourassa and White Streets still exist in their original locations. What was then named State Street is now Southfield Road, and Lafforter was renamed LeBlanc Street. Grandport continued to be the center of Ecorse Township for many years, but the little village was never incorporated. As the years passed, people stopped calling the commercial center Grandport and started calling it Ecorse, after the township's name. Gradually, the name Grandport faded into Ecorse history.

For many years, the area would be known as Ecorse Township. The name was derived from a term the early French settlers used. The name Ecorse Creek, whose two branches form much of the boundaries for present-day Lincoln Park, came from an early French name for the waterway, Riviere aux Echorches. The English translation is "River of Bark." The bark referred to here has two explanations. One, Native Americans would strip the bark off trees to build canoes. And two, Native tribes used the bark to wrap bodies of the dead before burial. On April 12, 1827, the Michigan Territorial Legislature created the Township of Ecorse, an American spelling of the French word. The entire Downriver section was incorporated by the Territorial Legislature into the Township of Ecorse, a huge tract that covered present-day Wyandotte, Ecorse, Lincoln Park, Allen Park, Melvindale, River Rouge, Southwest Detroit, Taylor and Southgate. The name served the area for several more decades, but for present residents of Ecorse Township and future Lincoln Parkers, changes were coming.

Opposite: This 1876 map shows how large Ecorse Township (established in 1827) was initially. It also illustrates the prevalence of the early ribbon farms running east and west as well as north and south from the area rivers. *Lincoln Park Historical Museum*.

Chapter 2

INITIAL DEVELOPMENT AND EARLY SETTLEMENT

By the latter half of the 1800s, the number of settlers in Western Ecorse Township called for the initial development of what could best be described as a business district at Fort Street and what was then called the St. Cosme Line (Southfield Road). One of the earliest settlers to build in the area was Herman Quandt. He opened a grocery market in 1899 at the crossroads. His name was used as a designation for the growing intersection, and a community called Quandt's Corners was born.

This development occurred because of the numerous families immigrating into the area. During the middle of the 1800s, many German immigrants purchased farms in the western section of Ecorse Township. Settlers of French descent, who had been in the area for several decades and had established their farms near the Detroit and Rouge Rivers, began moving inland. The district became a melting pot of the two nationalities as they came together in present-day Lincoln Park. Early area families of German descent included the Keppens, Raupps, Poraths, Quandts, Theecks, Schonfelds, Schonschecks and Wolfes. French family names included LeBlancs, Bondies, Monties, Bourassas, Drouillards, Cicottes and Laffertys. There were other early settlers outside of these two groups whose names also became well-known names; those include the Goodells, Millers and McQuades.

The Quandt name figured prominently in the pioneer history of the area. Herman Quandt was born in 1871 in his parents' log cabin, which stood on the family farm on the corner of Allen Road and Old Pepper Road

The Herman C. Quandt house was built in 1906 at the corner of St. Cosme Line (Southfield Road) and Fort Street. The structure was moved to Fort Park and Philomene in 1925, when Fort Street was straightened. Sitting on the porch is Philomene Goodell. From left to right on the steps are Noreen Mullins, Bernice McQuade and Forest Hinch, and to the right of the steps is "Derby" Herman Smith, a bartender at Quandt's Saloon. *Lincoln Park Historical Museum.*

(Outer Drive). Quandt married Mary O. Goodell in 1888, and they had four children. One of the area's first businessmen, Quandt initially opened a saloon in a wooden building leased from David LeBlanc on the northeast corner of Fort Street and St. Cosme Line (Southfield Road). In 1908, he built a new structure that became a community center of activities.

Quandt's West Side Inn or Saloon was located on what is now the center of the Fort Street and Southfield intersection. The structure was a meeting place for many early settlers and pioneers. The second floor was used for square dancing and, later, for village council meetings. When Fort Street was cut through to Champagne Road, the building was moved, and in later years, it was used as a city hall. At one point, it contained the area library. The building now stands on Fort Street just south of Southfield Road and is presently the frame for the Painters Supply building.

Built in 1908, Herman Quandt's West Side Inn was a landmark in the area for many years. Initially located at what is today Southfield Road and Fort Street, it was the center of the community's social and civic life when the intersection was known as Quandt's Corners. *Lincoln Park Historical Museum.*

The Raupp family made a major impact in those early years. Due to revolution and unrest in the German states during the mid-1800s, the family sought freedom in the United States. Matthias Raupp and his family settled in Brooklyn, New York, when they first arrived, but following his wife's death, the family made its way to Michigan, specifically Ecorse Township. He purchased land for a farm near Pepper Road (Outer Drive) and Dix Avenue.

Matthias Raupp died just prior to 1900, leaving two sons, Gustave and Matthias Jr., in the Downriver area. Gustave and Alexis Salliotte of Ecorse founded the Salliotte and Raupp Lumber Company. Matthias Raupp Jr. continued to live on the family farm in what is today Lincoln Park. He died in 1937, leaving two sons, William and Matthias III. William "Bill" Raupp, born in 1874, purchased property near the family homestead and became a prominent figure in the growing area. William married Anne, and they had three children.

Early on, William was very civic minded. He was elected to serve on the Board of Township School District No. 5 in 1909 at Strowig School, which is the school he attended growing up. In the 1920s, Raupp built a home at 469

Top: Matthias Raupp arrived in what would become Lincoln Park in 1878. He built this log house and the outbuildings at the corner of Dix Avenue and Pepper Road (Outer Drive). Pictured from left to right are Matthias, William, Matthias Jr., Ann, Rose and Minnie Schonfeld Raupp. *Lincoln Park Historical Museum.*

Bottom: The lumberyard of the Salliotte and Raupp Lumber Company was not far from where the border of Lincoln Park would eventually be. The operation serviced a huge need for the area and was located near the Detroit River and Ecorse Creek in what was then Ecorse Township and today is the city of Ecorse. *Lincoln Park Historical Museum.*

Raupp Place. He was one of the leaders who pushed for the incorporation of Lincoln Park as a village in 1921, was elected village president in 1923 and became the first elected mayor of Lincoln Park when it was incorporated as a city in 1925. He was elected mayor again in 1929 and then served on the city council for twelve years. William Raupp was a charter member of the Lincoln Park Exchange Club, established in 1925, and served on the board of the State Savings Bank, the first bank to be established in the community. Raupp School was named for him, as was Raupp Place, a street near the site where he was born, lived and died. He passed away in 1948 at the age of seventy-four.

Another family that made its mark in the pioneer days of the area was the LeBlanc family. Descended from early French settlers, Pierre LeBlanc was deeded a section of land by the Potawatomi tribe in 1790. That first "ribbon farm" ran from the Detroit River into an area that is now known as Lincoln Park. Early family tales included talk of spearing muskrats and hauling in nets full of fish from the clear, unpolluted waters of the Detroit River. Abraham LeBlanc was the son of Pierre and his wife, Teresa. Abraham married Phyllis Perry around 1850, had eleven children and built a house in Ecorse Township. He served on the first Ecorse Township School Board and was a township highway commissioner. One of the couple's eleven children was Richard LeBlanc, who would go on to be a major part of early Lincoln Park history.

Born on December 17, 1853, in a log cabin built by his father, Abraham, Richard lived to see the evolution of the area from a wooded pioneer frontier into the much more developed and modern city of Lincoln Park. At the age of 23, he moved into what is today Lincoln Park and eventually built a house in the space where Fort Street and LeBlanc Street now meet. From that moment until his death at 107, he became what many would describe as the area's historian. His memory told of a time when the land was nothing but woods and the only roads were Goddard, Champaign, Fort Street and St. Cosme Line (Southfield Road). In his youth, he saw Wyandot and Fox Indians camped in the woods and the trading of woven baskets for bread that took place. When interviewed about the changes he saw in his lifetime, Richard related that he grew up with "no markets in the old days and had to live off the land. We ate pork fat and were glad to get it and it tasted good. But the land couldn't support America's population today. Machinery made a better and easier living possible."

Richard helped survey a portion of Fort Street and was on the crew that built the first bridge over the Rouge River. He worked at a sawmill for a

This house, built by Richard LeBlanc, sat in the middle of the intersection of present-day Fort Street and LeBlanc Street. It burned down in the early 1920s when the fire truck ran out of gas. When the fire engine finally arrived on the scene, firefighters found that the hydrant was frozen. *Lincoln Park Historical Museum.*

while, but mainly, he worked at farming and threshing. The first house he built burned down in the 1920s, right around the time that Lincoln Park was incorporated as a village. There was no fire department yet, and the Village of Ecorse Fire Department was summoned from quite a distance. The engine ran out of gas at the Ecorse Creek Bridge, and by the time it arrived at the house, it was discovered that the fire hydrant was frozen. Richard built a new house on the same site (3936 Fort Street). When Fort Street was extended, the structure was moved over to the corner.

Samuel LeBlanc, born in 1852 and Richard's brother, had a similar story line. He left Grandport in 1879, three years after his brother, to settle in present-day Lincoln Park. He built a log cabin initially and then, in 1892, replaced the cabin with a house at 2884 Fort Street. He farmed the acres around the house, and for many years, his prized possession was a shoulder yoke originally used by his father to carry water from the Detroit River. Samuel used the yoke to carry water from his well to his house and to the cows on his farm. Samuel lived to see the area grow from a crossroads community into a well-established city. He saw Fort Street when it was a cow path, and he lived at a time when the business district was composed of a grocery store and a saloon. Samuel farmed until 1921, when the LeBlanc farm was sold and subdivided, at which point he retired. He served as trustee on the township board of education for seventeen years and was very active in improvement associations when the area became known as Lincoln Park. Samuel LeBlanc died in 1936 at the LeBlanc Homestead. The house still stands but was added onto the 1960s in order to incorporate a business structure. The property is presently for sale.

Samuel's son, Joseph, was born in the family home and continued to live there until he got married. As his family grew, they stayed in the house to take care of his father. Joseph worked for the Lincoln Park School System his entire career. He was the building engineer at several school buildings, including Goodell School, Raupp School and LeBlanc School, named for his uncle Richard LeBlanc. Joseph retired in 1956 and became active in the Wyandotte and Lincoln Park Knights of Columbus and the St. Henry Ushers' Club and Holy Name Society. He played in the Wyandotte Knights' Band and led his own dance orchestra, LeBlanc's Rhythm Band, in the early 1920s. Joseph LeBlanc passed away in 1970 in Lincoln Park.

Samuel's daughter, Florence, became a valuable force for the cause of local history. She was born in 1883 in the log cabin mentioned above built by her father at Fort Street and Champaign. She married Edward Bodary, and

The Samuel LeBlanc House, built in the 1890s, still stands near Fort Street and Champaign. Samuel originally constructed a log cabin on the site in 1879, and as his family grew, a larger house was erected. The structure has been modified to include a business. *Lincoln Park Historical Museum.*

they had three children. Later in life, in 1954, she joined a group of history-minded Lincoln Park residents in forming the Lincoln Park Historical Society, one of the first to be established Downriver. She became the most active member and was elected director of the society at the first meeting. Using her influence in the area, Florence was able to generate a passion in local residents for donating items of historical interest. She also helped compile numerous histories of area pioneer families, including many pages of genealogical data relating to those early families.

Another member of the LeBlanc clan who helped in developing the area was David A. LeBlanc. David built a saloon, which became known as the Patron Hall, in 1890. The business was part of the growing area known as Quandt's Corners and was located on the northeast corner of Fort Street and St. Cosme Line (Southfield Road). The lumber used to build the structure came from local trees that had been cut at the Raupp Sawmill located on the Detroit River and Ecorse Creek. Eventually, the building was rented to Herman Quandt and Clem Bourassa, who continued to operate it as a saloon. When Fort Street was widened, the structure was moved to Southfield Road across from city hall.

While there, it became a speakeasy due to Prohibition and catered to Pennsylvania Railroad construction workers known as gandy dancers. *Gandy dancer* was a slang term used for early railroad workers (they were called section hands) in the United States who laid and maintained railroad tracks in the years before the work was done by machine. Section hands were called gandy dancers for the synchronized "dancing" movements of the men using a long "lining" bar, called a gandy. The name is said to be based on the name of the company that manufactured the bars that helped to lever track rails into alignment. The team yanked the bars in unison to nudge the rail and tie sections back into place, often timed by the cadence of a song or chant. When Prohibition ended, the speakeasy closed down, and a furniture store took over the building. The structure is no longer standing.

Among the earliest families of French descent in the area were the Bondies. George and Ida Foley Bondie built a home on Fort Park Boulevard near Champaign Road in the late 1800s. The couple raised seven children in the house while George managed a grocery store with his brother in Delray. The house was razed in 1918 and replaced with a brick structure. Some of the property owned by the Bondies was donated for the building of Goodell School in 1918.

Goodell is a pioneer name of major importance in terms of the development of the area. Elijah Goodell settled in the area from upstate

Top: Built in 1890 by David LeBlanc, this saloon and store became an integral part of the growing settlement. Located on the northeast corner of what is today Fort Street and Southfield Road, the business was rented and then purchased by Herman Quandt, who continued to operate it as a saloon. *Lincoln Park Historical Museum.*

Bottom: In the background is the David LeBlanc Saloon. Pictured in front, from left to right, are Lewis Porath, Herman Wolf, owner D.A. LeBlanc and C. Wolf. The structure was moved to a location across from city hall when Fort Street was widened. The building has now been lost to history. *Lincoln Park Historical Museum.*

This house was built by George Bondie in the late 1800s. The Bondie family farm was near Fort Street and Champaign Road. In 1918, the structure was replaced by the new brick Goodell School. *Lincoln Park Historical Museum.*

New York in the late 1790s. He built a log cabin near the Detroit River in Ecorse Township and worked as a limekiln operator on Grosse Ile. In 1852, his grandson Cleophus purchased 120 acres from Native Americans in the area and built a four-room farmhouse. Cleophus married Philomene Riopelle, and the couple raised five children at 2136 Fort Park Boulevard. Each child was deeded 9 acres of land. The Goodell School, well known in the area, was named after Cleophus.

Mark Goodell was the youngest of the five children born to Cleophus and Philomene. Born in 1884, Mark was not only born at the family house on Fort Park Boulevard, but he also continued living there when he married Stella Frances "Lottie" Batchelor in 1916. The couple raised seven children there. Many of the area streets are named after the children. The Goodells were the first to have a telephone installed in their home. Mark purchased an automobile in the 1920s but never learned to drive. He hired a neighbor to chauffeur him around, but unbeknownst to Goodell, the neighbor was also using the vehicle at night to bootleg moonshine from the Ecorse River to Lincoln Park during Prohibition.

The Keppen family came to the Lincoln Park area from Germany in the mid-1800s. Henry Keppen built this house in the late 1800s on Pepper Road (Outer Drive). The structure was torn down in the mid-1900s. *Lincoln Park Historical Museum.*

Mark Goodell, after graduating from high school, attended the University of Detroit to study medicine. He decided against pursuing a career in medicine and shifted his attention to real estate development and local politics. Mark was elected president of the area school board in 1915. Then, in 1921, when Lincoln Park was incorporated as a village, he became the first president. He was instrumental in Lincoln Park becoming a city in 1925 and was elected mayor in 1927; he served through 1929.

August Keppen was a pioneer farmer whose family came to the area from Germany in the mid-1800s. He was born in 1862 in Ecorse Township. He married Anna Lindeman, and their children were Louis and Mamie. August served on the school board of Township District 10 when it was in its infancy. Louis was employed in the position of coal dealer by Gerisch Coal of Detroit. He also served as the first treasurer of Lincoln Park when it was first incorporated as a village in 1921. He passed away in 1933 at his home on Southfield Road just north of Fort Street. The house, located at 1324 State Street (Southfield Road), became R.C. Aleks & Son Funeral Home in the 1950s. The business is still in operation today.

In the early 1900s, there was an evolution taking place in terms of shopping experience. That evolution included a new format called the grocery store.

Instead of trying to offer a wide array under one roof, food began to be separated into its own specialty stores. In Lincoln Park, one of the early grocery and meat markets was owned and operated by Joseph Toleikis. The business was located on Fort Street and Arlington Street. Walking into Toleikis Grocery would have been a very different experience from today's chain grocery stores. The local grocery store owner in the early 1900s was a friend and a neighbor. Patrons came into the store not just to purchase items needed for the family but also to be social and discuss current events. Some of the owners might have extended a line of credit, and a required period would have been established for payment. The shelves at Toleikis were filled with staples and a few fancy items along with a large variety of locally grown fruits and vegetables. The availability of meat would also have been a huge draw for customers. Chain grocery stores really exploded on the scene in the 1930s and 1940s. Because of the chains' economies of scale and operational efficiency, many of the mom-and-pop grocery stores were forced to close. The Toleikis Grocery closed and was torn down in the 1920s when the Fort Street development took off. In 1927, after Fort Street had been widened, Toleikis built a new three-story brick building on the property. The old grocery had now been replaced by many new grocers along Fort Street, but that first store was a key building block in the area where it operated at a unique time of transition.

This view shows Southfield Road and the back of a row of businesses on Fort Street in the 1930s. The one solitary house in the foreground was built by Louis Keppen on land his father, August Keppen, purchased. The house was transformed into the R.C. Aleks & Son Funeral Home in the mid-1950s. *Lincoln Park Historical Museum.*

Left: One of the early grocery stores in what would become Lincoln Park. Joseph Toleikis ran this store on the northwest corner of Fort Street and Arlington. The business was torn down and replaced by a three-story Toleikis apartment and retail building in the 1920s that still stands today. *Lincoln Park Historical Museum.*

Below: Transportation in the early days of the area was often an impossible task. Dirt roads turned to mud in times of heavy rain. Wagon wheels and horse hooves do not travel well in thick, deep mud. Pictured here is Fort Street in 1911. *Lincoln Park Historical Museum.*

It is important to understand what it was like to travel from one place to another in those early days. One of the biggest headaches for the early settlers was simply the mud. Early accounts speak about a sticky clay-like "goo" that hampered travel to a great degree. Horse-drawn wagons often had their wheels sink in the mud all the way to the hub. The wheels would become so plastered that they would just slide and no longer turn. Florence Bodary, daughter of Samuel LeBlanc, related her memory of the 1880s, when a fisherman by the name of Toddy Drouillard would show up to her family house on the corner of Fort Street and Champaign and walk around with a wheelbarrow of sturgeon for sale because traveling was so difficult and those who got stuck might be interested in purchasing some fish. One newspaper account described the travel situation as late as 1912, around the time Fort Street was first paved: "Once a person left the pavement, especially during the spring months, travel was almost impossible." Bodary also reported that there was a traveling "peddler named Jake who was a Godsend to the community when we were unable to go shopping because of muddy roads." Samuel LeBlanc's son Joseph was interviewed about his earliest memories of the traveling conditions: "I remember in the spring of about 1900 when the telegraph company undertook the task of dismantling one of their lines. Two teams of horses hitched to a platform wagon carrying a 600-pound weight and the wheels were so clogged with mud they slid half the time."

For over two hundred years, one of the main travel routes through the area now known as Lincoln Park has been Fort Street. Not long after Detroit was founded in 1701, the French built a fortification. It was constructed in what is today downtown Detroit. Cadillac named the new settlement Fort Pontchartrain du Detroit to honor the French marine minister who approved his expedition. The French hoped to use the fort to build alliances with the Native Americans living in the Ohio valley in order to protect their interests in the region from British encroachment. It was not long before various tribes migrated to the Detroit area and established villages for trading. A trail, which had existed long before the establishment of Detroit, was used to reach the fort and eventually a growing community. Originally known as the "River Road," this trail, today known as Jefferson Avenue, was established and ran from Fort Pontchartrain southwest and south through the Downriver area. Over time, Fort Pontchartrain fell into disrepair, and during the American Revolution, British Captain Richard Lernoult ordered that a new fort be constructed. The structure was renamed Fort Detroit in 1805. A map from that time shows the establishment of "Fort Street," which ran outward from the fort and through what is today Lincoln Park. The road was only dirt up until 1912. As industry moved into the area and housing developed, the need for improved roads brought about the paving and widening of Fort Street.

A decade into the 1900s saw the long-standing farms in the area give way to subdivisions and the beginnings of real estate development as suburbanization began to move outward from Detroit. One of the earliest moves in this direction in what would later be called Lincoln Park was a real estate venture known as the Suburban City Company (SCC). The SCC was a real estate venture established in 1912 in association with the Suburban Motor Car Company (SMCC).

The short-lived Suburban Motor Car Company (1911–13) is today just a footnote in the long saga of automotive history. Yet it became part of a fascinating chapter of that history that would include such disparate elements as the Seven Little Buffaloes, a mayor of Bad Axe, the Ecorse River, a noted landscape architect and a model village, the first Lincoln Park Subdivisions and the Checker Cab Co. If the SMCC had been successful and the building plans for the area had come to fruition, the City of Lincoln Park would have had a very different destiny and layout.

The story of the SMCC begins with William A. DeSchaum (original name Schaum), an automotive design engineer, who started the DeSchaum Motor Company in Buffalo, New York (1908–10). The company, noted for the DeSchaum's distinctive high wheel rims, struggled in a market of better and cheaper cars; some would argue that DeSchaum was more of a dreamer than a businessman. In early 1910, he whimsically re-dubbed his car the "Seven Little Buffaloes," but the name change did not help business, and before long the fledgling company went under.

The same year, DeSchaum moved west to Detroit, where he met up with Frank Farnham and William Lankin, a former mayor of Bad Axe. Lankin became president of the new enterprise, with DeSchaum as general manager and vice president, Farnham as secretary and O.B. Bachman as treasurer; together they formed a new DeSchaum Motor Car Company to produce DeSchaum's roadster, the Suburban Limited. After producing just a handful of the prototype cars in two styles of roadster, the DeSchaum Motor Car Company was reorganized in September 1911, with the same officers, into the Suburban Motor Car Company, now with ambitious plans for a new industrial community on extensive acreage in nearby Ecorse Township. According to press announcements in the *New York Times* as well as many automotive journals at that time (*The Automobile*; *Motor*; *Motor*

NUMBER 57

SHARES

Suburban City Company

INCORPORATED UNDER THE LAWS OF MICHIGAN

FULL PAID CAPITAL STOCK, $500,000 NON-ASSESSABLE

SHARES $100 EACH

This Certifies that Thomas is the owner of Four Shares of the Capital Stock of Suburban City Company transferable only on the books of this Corporation in person or by Attorney upon surrender of this Certificate properly endorsed.

IN WITNESS WHEREOF, the said Corporation has caused this Certificate to be signed by its duly authorized officers and its Corporate Seal to be hereunto affixed this third day of May A.D.

SECRETARY PRESIDENT

Starting in 1911, stock was sold to raise money for the ill-fated Suburban City Company. The plan was to build a "company city" or neighborhood where employees and management of the Suburban Motor Car Company would be housed in what was dubbed a "Garden Village." It was an ambitious plan, but for many reasons, it failed. *Lincoln Park Historical Museum.*

World; *Iron Trade*; *Iron Age*; *Automotive Industries*; *Motor Age*; *Accessories & Garage Journal*), the new Suburban Motor Car Company was designed to be an impressive complex of factory buildings with direct access, via the Ecorse River, to the Detroit River and to the Michigan Central Railroad lines that ran through to the city from the south, with an adjacent model "garden village" where the employees of the SMCC would live. (Note: the factory location in Detroit where the first Suburban vehicles were manufactured in 1911 is yet a mystery.)

At the same time, the officers separately formed the Suburban City Company Real Estate firm, which shared SMCC's Whitney Building offices in downtown Detroit. The real estate enterprise was established to promote the planned development of the 240 acres of Ecorse Township into the model village to be known as "Suburban City." The SMCC's ambitious scheme for a "garden village" was described in the trade journal, *Parks and Cemeteries and Landscape Gardening*, of November 1912. This article also

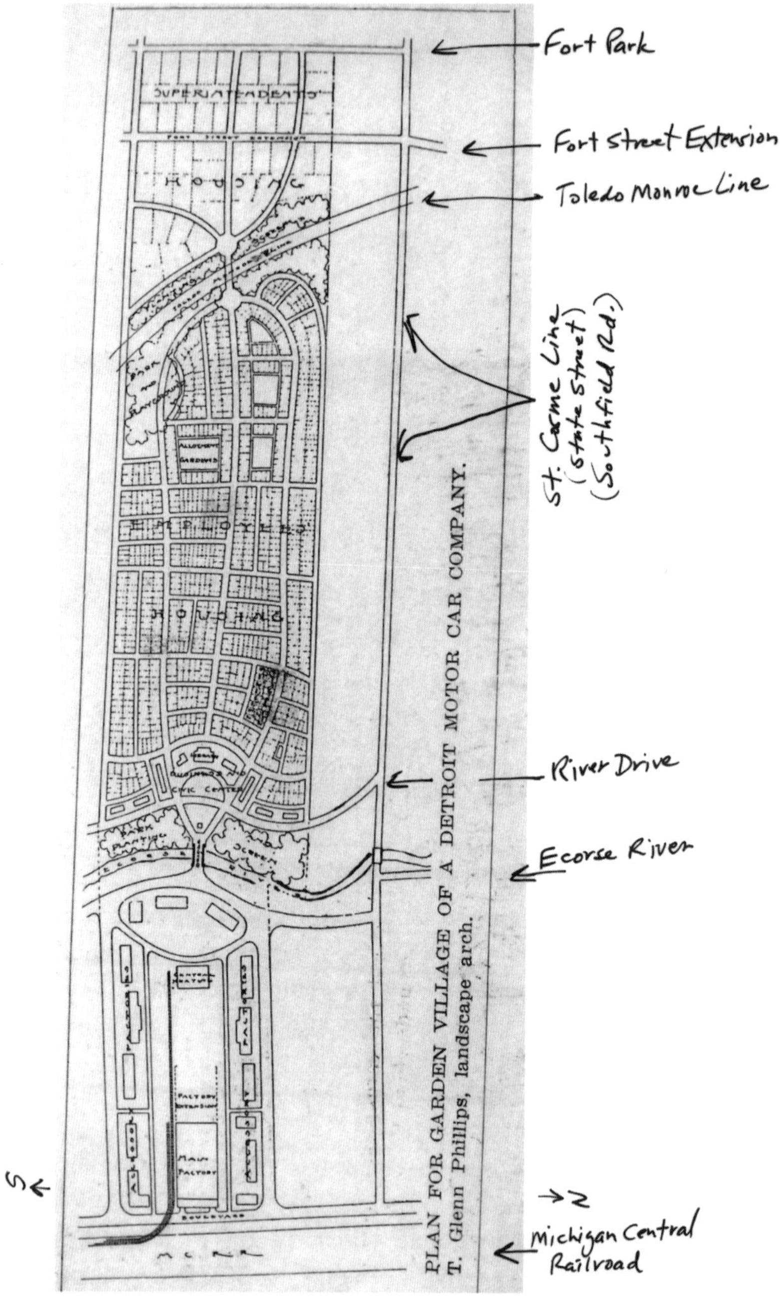

This detailed design, prepared in 1912, was presented to promote the development of 240 acres into a "garden village" known as "Suburban City." The unique detailed design for the "garden village" was rendered by noted landscape architect T. Glenn Phillips. *Lincoln Park Historical Museum.*

to the surrounding lots, on which larger gardens may be developed by those so inclined in the adjoining lots.

Beyond the employees' housing area, the property is adjusted to the needs of men with larger income, such as superintendents or heads of department who desire more ample ground, not only as a setting to their homes, but for cultivation as gardens.

Provisions are made for the creation of park areas which serve as screens between the several sections of the property and for recreation. On the banks of the Ecorse River plantings are made which will not only alleviate the saturated and unhealthy conditions of the soil, but create a beauty spot, a rendezvous for boating and water sports.

A larger space is devoted to planting on the boundary between the two main housing areas, accessible to both and yet forming a screen from the electric railroad and a dividing line between the sections. Here a park is planned in a grove already existing.

Everything is arranged to produce a congruous whole and the factories are grouped artistically. The design of the employees' houses is controlled in order to form a unified composition—English half-timber cottages—which differ in individual design but are harmonious in the group. The heating and lighting is from a central plant, while the water supply, sewerage and wiring are all carried in common underground conduits.

The perspective study for this development is already completed and detailed plans are being finished which will be followed immediately by the actual construction. T. Glenn Phillips, landscape architect, of Detroit, has been retained to prepare a comprehensive scheme. He will have not only direct supervision of the general design but also will have under his control the actual construction, the architectural design of the houses, which will be built by the company and rented or sold, the layout and planting of parks and playgrounds, and the general engineering details such as streets, water supply, sewerage and lighting.

To many the significance of this action on the part of a large manufacturing concern is not clear. It is simply another indication that manufacturers as well as other classes of great producers are awaking to the fact that a more perfect product depends not wholly on more perfect machinery but also on more perfect conservation of energy, particularly human energy; that the factory town of the past with its closely built houses, its filthy alleys and other disease breeders cannot bring healthy and efficient workmen to the factory. They realize that not only must their factories be so placed that the minimum of time and energy is lost in shipping and inter-

> *factory movements, but also that the relation of the factory to the housing areas must be perfectly sane, not too distant for accessibility, nor too near for reasons of sanitation and health. The realize that the provision of more carefully planned and related streets and houses is reflected in a greater human efficiency as well as finer personnel, which will create about the plant an esprit-de-corps, which has proved the making of so many large organizations.*
>
> *We have come, it seems, to an era which demands clearer, saner industrial thinking, which decrees that ruthless disregard of human interests, desires and life cannot continue, that such disregard eventually proves ruinous, and that the opposite course is not only more humane but far more successful financially.*

This description highlights the immense undertaking this project would have been in creating what truly would have been a city within a city. The legacy of the Suburban Motor Car Company and the Suburban City Company lives on in the form of the "what if" dreams of history and in one physical residual. A Google map search for "Suburban Street" reveals the width of Suburban Boulevard as planned out way back in 1912. In later years, that land was used to form extra-wide front lawns that few probably realize the significance of except for readers of this book.

In June 1913, Palmer joined the Partin Manufacturing Company and moved operations to Chicago, where they began producing the Partin-Palmer auto. Partin-Palmer in turn became the Commonwealth from 1915 until 1922. Commonwealth had developed a taxicab called the Mogul; after more reorganization, the Commonwealth evolved into the Checker Cab Company for its fleet production. Checker moved to Kalamazoo in April 1923. By 1924, Checker was producing four thousand units a year.

Little remains of the dreams of these men. When automobile production ceased, the Village of Ecorse annexed the portion of land from Southfield Road to Ecorse Creek. Then, in 1921, the Village of Lincoln Park absorbed the remaining section. The establishment of early real estate firms and the first subdivisions of land in Lincoln Park were led by the Farnham Brothers. Suburban Street in Ecorse, which was designed to be the wide central thoroughfare for the factory complex, remains as wide today, without most folks knowing why. It is interesting to imagine what this area of Ecorse Township and Lincoln Park might have developed into had the Suburban Motor Car Company been a success. History can be fickle. It was just a few years later when auto magnate Henry Ford arrived three miles down the road and began building his mammoth Rouge River plant; it was at that point that the soon-to-be Lincoln Park would swell with a population of auto workers of whom William A. DeSchaum had only dreamed. By the time 1921 rolled around, the locals and the steady influx of new residents were singing the praises of Mr. Henry Ford.

Chapter 3

INCORPORATION AND REAL ESTATE BOOM

As discussed in the previous chapter, in the 1910s, the long-standing farms of pioneer families were subdivided, and real estate became the newest and liveliest venture, a response to suburbanization and the availability of industrial jobs. The real estate boom struck Lincoln Park head-on through the 1920s, although the seeds of change had been planted a few years earlier. The Farnham Brothers agency was founded in 1913. Maurice Levy, another early realtor of note, largely focused on developing the central business district, leaving the residential plots and most subdivisions to the competition. Levy's business grew from a simple stand by the side of the road in 1915 to a very prominent central building at Fort and State Streets by 1923. Subdivisions were bought up and sold by nearly two dozen realtors before the Great Depression hit in October 1929. While real estate quickly became a lucrative business, and some agents stayed for only a brief time, most realtors were responsible-minded and dedicated to seeing the community grow, of which many were a part.

The most significant building venture nearby was the Ford Motor Company factory on the Rouge River. This colossal undertaking had a major impact on the development of the area. The factory began hiring upon opening in 1918. By the 1930s, over 100,000 people were employed at the Ford plant, the world's largest manufacturing complex. A decade earlier, Henry Ford's attractive five-dollar-a-day wages and eight-hour days—and plentiful jobs—began to draw an increasing number of migrants to the Detroit area from out of state and foreign shores. Riverfront steel mills and

Significant development started to occur in 1913 and into the 1920s with what some historians call the "real estate boom." It was around that time when a transition from a farming community to housing neighborhoods and business-oriented development took place. With nearby industry opportunities in the area, Lincoln Park was viewed as a desirable place to buy a house. *Lincoln Park Historical Museum.*

shipbuilding provided other nearby opportunities. New suburbs sprang up around the newly motorized city, offering newcomers—many of whom were recent veterans of the First World War—abundant opportunities for work and community.

Around this same time, in early 1920, a number of area residents met in the Strowig School, forming the Lincoln Park Improvement Association, and voted on a plan that would establish the Village of Lincoln Park. According to some historians, the Farnham Brothers had introduced the name "Lincoln Park" in 1913 simply because they liked the way it sounded. Another account claims that it was village president Mark Goodell who brought the name up in conversation (more on the name below). Whatever the case, the decision to use the name and to form as an organized village was now before the people. The proposal presented the following to the area residents: whether to approve the incorporation of a new village to be named Lincoln Park from a section of Ecorse Township. The vote, which was township-wide, was successful by a margin of 1,561 to 1,077. Soon after the March 11 vote, another election was held to create the Charter Commission, tasked with creating the village's new charter, which would then be presented to the State of Michigan.

Thus, the process began of creating a new community out of a long-standing territory of farm families. The section selected for incorporation (as described in detail on the March 11, 1921 ballot) was bounded on the north by Pepper Road (Outer Drive) at Raupp Road and the North Branch of the Ecorse River; on the east by the Ecorse River and Gohl Road; on the south by Goddard Road and the South Branch of the Ecorse River; and on the west by a zigzag pattern incorporating Fort Street, Champaign Road, Raupp Road and St. Cosme Road returning to Pepper Road. The first village officials included Mark A. Goodell, president; Floyd Harrison, clerk; Louis Keppen, treasurer; and James Green, George Shanley, Harry H. Sharpe, Fred J. White, Delbert Wilbur and Harry J. Timm as commissioners.

Over a four-year period, the Village of Lincoln Park mushroomed from a population of three hundred in 1921 to over nine thousand in early 1925. During those years, several additional square miles were annexed to the village, and the populace approved the incorporation of Lincoln Park as a city. In a vote held on April 6, 1925, the populace voted to approve the new city charter, and the following officials were the first to serve the newly formed City of Lincoln Park: William Raupp, mayor; Floyd W. Harrison, clerk; Arthur C. Nieman, treasurer; Floyd S. Flynn, judge; Anton Eisner, constable; and Arthur Weston, Edward Davis, Reinhold Nass, Albert Babbitt, George Shanley and Louis J. Keppen serving as councilmen.

Frank Farnham, one of the real estate brothers mentioned earlier, was a native of Fenton, Michigan. He came to the area in 1913 and was part of the organization of the Suburban Motor Car Company. To facilitate the automotive venture, Farnham purchased land from St. Cosme Line (Southfield Road) south to the vicinity of Emmons Boulevard and from Michigan Central Railroad west to Fort Street. Suburban Boulevard, in what is today the city of Ecorse, was designed to be the main thoroughfare. The enterprise folded after just two years. The Village of Ecorse annexed the portion of land from the railroad to Ecorse Creek, and then in 1921, when Lincoln Park became a village, the new entity incorporated the remaining section. Farnham remained in the area for many years and helped with the early real estate development. His legacy lives on in the city in the form of a street named after him, and depending on which origin story is true, many believe he is the one responsible for giving Lincoln Park its name.

The story of the naming of Lincoln Park deserves a bit more detail. Russell Murdock, who served as the first engineer of the Village of Lincoln Park, recalled that the Farnham brothers gave their subdivision the name

After Lincoln Park was incorporated as a village in 1921, two lots and a building were gifted to the new entity by G.W. Zanger, a prominent Detroit resident, for the purpose of council meetings. Located at 1035 Lincoln Boulevard, this building was the first city hall for the Village of Lincoln Park. It was torn down in the early 1950s. *Lincoln Park Historical Museum.*

"Lincoln Park" simply because they "wanted a title for their development in Ecorse Township and decided Lincoln Park was a nice name." The brothers, after getting their subdivisions underway, decided to set aside a parcel of land for a park. They promised to give this parcel to the township for this express purpose. The park was to be situated at what is today Lincoln and Electric Streets. No deed was ever provided or pursued by the township. In 1916, the United States was hit by a serious coal strike, and there was little to no coal for purchase that winter. Searching for fuel, residents began to cut down trees in the area. On the land that the Farnham brothers had promised to donate for a park, large numbers of trees were cut down. During a trip to inspect their subdivisions, the brothers discovered that the trees on the promised parcel had been, for the most part, cleared. They complained to township authorities and threatened to withdraw the gift if the people responsible were not brought to justice. The park was never developed, but the name Lincoln Park lives on.

However, the above story about how the city got its name is not the only one that has been recorded. Frances Goodell, the wife of Mark Goodell, the first president of the Village of Lincoln Park, always refuted the Farnham brothers' version. She claimed, until the day she died, that her husband was responsible for the name. In a 1971 interview, Mrs. Goodell claimed the following: "Several years before Lincoln Park was incorporated, my husband had visited Chicago and was so impressed by a park in the city called Lincoln Park. When 'Quandt's Corners' decided to break away from Ecorse Township and become a village, he suggested that Lincoln Park be used as the new name." No matter which version is accurate, the name Lincoln Park has served the area now for over one hundred years and will seemingly always be associated with historical intrigue.

With the incorporation of Lincoln Park as a village and then a few years later as a city, official service groups were founded: a city council, police department, fire department and district court. Of course, the transition to village status called for a location for village officials to meet and discuss the future of this new entity. A building and two lots were gifted to the village by G.W. Zanger, a prominent Detroit resident. The council chamber would be located at 1035 Lincoln Boulevard at Electric. The building would not be in use for very long, as the council decided to begin meeting at the former Quandt's Saloon in 1924. The building on Lincoln Boulevard was used for many purposes over the years: temporary housing for several families during the Depression, a storage shed for the department of public works and a band shell for concerts. The structure also made several moves. In 1953, it was moved from Lincoln Boulevard to Howard and Cicotte Streets and used by the police department. The building was torn down in the 1950s to make way for the I-75 freeway.

The second city hall, the former Quandt's Saloon mentioned previously, was originally located at the end of Fort Street, on St. Cosme Line (Southfield Road). When Fort Street was extended and widened, the building was moved to the northwest corner of St. Cosme Line and Fort Street, and then finally to 2030 Fort Street. Through the years, the structure served as a city hall, a Wayne County Library Branch and Times Furniture Company. Over the years, the building was incorporated into the Painter's Supply store structure, which still stands today.

Lincoln Park government moved to a new city hall in 1936. The newly constructed building was part of the Federal Works Progress Administration projects in the Downriver area. The design of the building incorporated a U-shape where all city services, including the police and fire departments, could be located under the same roof. The Art Deco building included a fifty-foot tower for drying fire hoses. The facility was dedicated in 1936 with

This version of the Lincoln Park City Hall originally stood at 2030 Fort Street near Southfield Road. The building was constructed in 1908 and served as a tavern when the area was known as Quandt's Corners. The structure was moved twice after Fort Street was widened and then incorporated into what is today the Painter's Supply building. *Lincoln Park Historical Museum.*

a lot of celebration and excitement. A parade of civic, fraternal, military and social organizations walked the street in celebration. The mayor at the time, Jasper Howard, accepted keys from the Works Progress Administration administrator, and immediately following the presentation, there was dancing on Fort Park Boulevard.

The very first "Lincoln Park Day" was held on July 4, 1921, just six days after the Village of Lincoln Park was incorporated. It was sponsored by the Lincoln Park Improvement Association and the new village officials. The event was a celebratory picnic located at Fort Street at St. Cosme Line (Southfield Road) with ball games, races, hot dogs and fireworks. The second Lincoln Park Day and the first boat trip was held on Thursday, July 10, 1924, sponsored by the Lincoln Park Board of Commerce. The steamer *Tashmoo* was chartered and picked up picnickers at the foot of State Street (Southfield Road) in Ecorse. The destination was Sugar Island opposite the south end of Grosse Ile—at that time one of the most popular resorts on the river. The third Lincoln Park Day took place in 1925. The steamer *Tashmoo* this

Where the present Lincoln Park City Hall sits used to be the home of the public works, the city police and the fire department. The building was constructed in 1935 for $80,000. It was one of the largest Works Progress Administration projects in the Downriver area. *Lincoln Park Historical Museum.*

time took residents of the newly incorporated City of Lincoln Park from the State Street dock to Tashmoo Park on Harsen's Island at the St. Clair Flats. Although the boat ride took two hours and forty-five minutes, the partygoers seemed to enjoy the leisurely trip up the Detroit River across Lake St. Clair to the park. Many outdoor games and events were enjoyed by the Lincoln Parkers that day, along with its casino and dance pavilion, but the big event was the drawing for a new 1925 Ford Touring Car that had been purchased by the Exchange Club. The day's attendance was recorded at 1,004 adults and 309 children.

Sometime before the 1940s, Lincoln Park Day shifted venues, and the day was treated as a holiday for the entire city where much of the populace, including the mayor and city council, spent the day at Bob-Lo Island. According to former Lincoln Park patrolman Donald Wallace in his book *Growing Up in Simpler Times*:

> *Weeks prior to the holiday, most businesses would display colorful window signs of the date and place of the one-day holiday. Most city businesses*

> *would close as well as the city's only bank at Fort and O'Connor.... The first sight of the huge Bob-Lo boat began our hearts pounding with excitement of the day to come...The Mayor and City Council members that were present would have foot races while inside a burlap potato sack, horse shoe pitching, softball games and all to the sound of music and dancing coming from the large covered pavilion.... The cruise back was quiet compared to the early ride of the morning...Finally docking in Wyandotte and then began the long walk home to Lincoln Park and talking of next year and another "Lincoln Park Day."*

In 1921, the Lincoln Park Police Department began when the village hired its first officer, Joseph Rowe. Within a few years, the department had acquired its first vehicles: two Studebakers, two motorcycles and a Model-T. The first building that housed the police department stood across from the city hall on a tract of land that is presently in the middle of Southfield Road. It is now a parking lot. As the community grew and the city hall complex was completed, including space for the police department, the structure was taken down. Then, in 1955, the police department moved one more time into a new, state-of-the-art headquarters located on Cleophus Street. The construction of the building was funded by the sale of the Dix Avenue and Southfield Road corner to Sears and Roebuck.

One of the earliest members of the police force was Preston Tucker. Tucker grew up in Lincoln Park and attended Detroit's Cass Technical High School. His mother was a schoolteacher in Ecorse Township and later the Lincoln Park public school system. Tucker possessed innate mechanical skills and was known to tinker with his motorcycle and squad car in order to make them go faster. In later years, Tucker became famous for his automobile company and his "Tucker '48" model. It was one of the most unique vehicles ever designed and built.

As envisioned by Tucker himself, the "Tucker Torpedo" represented quite a departure from the standard automobiles offered by the Big Three automakers. Long, low and substantially wider than other large cars that were then available, with sleek lines reminiscent of a rocket, it had doors that slid up into the roof and six chrome-plated exhaust pipes. Its unique safety features included a center headlight mounted directly in front that moved with the front wheels to illuminate the road as the car made a turn, a windshield made of shatterproof glass, seat belts, disc brakes and a heavily padded dashboard to protect front-seat passengers in the event of a collision.

The Lincoln Park Police Department was initially housed in this building (shown in 1926), which stood in the middle of present-day Southfield Road on land that is now a parking lot. In the picture is Floyd Crichton (*left*) and Preston Tucker. *Lincoln Park Historical Museum.*

In terms of engineering, the "Tucker Torpedo" was a unique vehicle. It boasted a gigantic, fuel-injected, six-cylinder engine mounted in the rear that its creator claimed could hit a top speed of 130 miles per hour, maintain a cruising speed of 100 miles per hour and deliver an astonishing 35 miles-per-gallon gas mileage. In addition, it sported a revolutionary power delivery system of "hydraulic torque converters" that Tucker said would eliminate the need for a clutch, transmission, drive shaft and differential.

But while his designs and safety innovations were pioneering, Tucker's business model was lacking. Car manufacturing had contracted during the Great Depression, and by the late 1940s, only a handful of companies remained, rooted in a culture that valued corporate prudence over individual genius. By the mid-1950s, Ford, General Motors and Chrysler manufactured 95 percent of American cars.

According to some industry experts, Tucker refused to cede creative control to businessmen who could have made the Tucker '48 commercially viable. The truth of this is, of course, up for debate. Instead, he attempted to raise money through unconventional means, including selling dealership rights for a car that did not even exist yet. The Securities and Exchange Commission investigated, and he was taken to court on charges of fraud.

Although he was acquitted in 1950, he went bankrupt. Only fifty-one vehicles were manufactured. Tucker died a few years later from lung cancer. Today, forty-seven of his vehicles are still in existence, and they are considered to be among the most sought-after automobile collection pieces.

The Lincoln Park Fire Department was founded in 1925. Prior to this, emergency services were provided by the Ecorse Township Department. During the first few years of their existence, the fire and police departments shared the same building. When a new city hall was built on Southfield Road in 1936, the fire department took up residence in the back of that building, located on the southwest corner of Fort Park Boulevard and Southfield Road. In 1963, a new two-story, 13,500-square-foot facility was built on the southwest corner of Fort Park Boulevard and Cleophus Street. The fire department finally had a home of its own.

Incorporation as a city also brought municipal court services to the area. Judge Roy Cicotte played a pivotal role in developing Lincoln Park's standing in the legal arena, and he also participated in many community organizations. Because of his efforts, his name lives on in many forms throughout Lincoln Park. Cicotte was born on July 21, 1921, in Ecorse, Michigan, just prior to the incorporation of Lincoln Park as a village. He attended Lincoln Park Schools and graduated in 1937. He attended Wayne State University, the Detroit College of Business and Detroit College of Law, where he completed his doctor of jurisprudence. During World War II, Roy served in the U.S. Army Air Force.

He began his law practice in Allen Park and Melvindale in 1957 and was appointed Allen Park's city attorney. He served as a judge in the Twenty-Fifth District Court in Lincoln Park for twenty years. In 1989, the court building at 1475 Cleophus Parkway was named in his honor. He was active in the American Legion, serving as state commander in 1987. Cicotte was an honorary member of the 40 and 8 Club. (The 40 and 8 Club was established as a charitable and patriotic organization by veterans of World War I in 1920. The name refers to French railroad boxcars that were marked "40/8," which indicated they could hold either forty soldiers or eight horses.) Cicotte Street, which today runs through Lincoln Park, Ecorse and Allen Park, was named for the Cicotte family, a pioneer French-Canadian family who settled in the area before 1800.

As stated earlier, the real estate boom struck Lincoln Park head-on through the 1920s. Beginning in 1921, the Village of Lincoln Park was dotted with nicer brick building businesses: Great Atlantic and Pacific Tea Company, a restaurant, a drugstore, a hardware store and the State Savings Bank, to name a few. And there was a real thrust at that time for further development. The Lincoln Park Land Company was prominently located on the corner of Fort Street and State Street (Southfield Road). A huge billboard faced those who were driving south on Fort Street toward State Street. The billboard was an advertisement by B.A. Horger highlighting opportunities for real estate investment and the availability of "vacant acreage for improvement or even for factory site use."

Maurice Levy was a huge force behind the transformation that was to come. Born in Chicago, he moved to Detroit in 1915. Backed by investors from Detroit, he became a real estate agent for the St. Cosme Land Company and turned an eye to Southwest Wayne County as he looked to "attract workers from all West side plants in Detroit [and provide] homes for new employees in [Henry Ford's] Eagle Boat plant." One of the first parcels Levy purchased in the area was a strip of land from brothers August and Henry Keppen. It ran from Southfield Road to Montie Road and from Fort Street to Lafayette Boulevard. Thus began the formal subdividing of Lincoln Park. Always the optimist, Levy foresaw a great future for the area because of its location: "All of the big Detroit and downriver industries are at its door, yet it'll be the home of a fine class of people. Sure, we've gone in debt to install streets and sewers and other improvements. But now they're in, and the taxes are bound to go down as the debt is paid off."

His headquarters was the first modern brick building in the Village of Lincoln Park. He became the sole owner of his own firm in three years. Because of Levy's vision, the first water lines were installed throughout the district and the area's first brick buildings were constructed. In 1925, Levy built the Park Theater. He always had faith in Lincoln Park's future. At the peak of his activity, he had sixty salesmen on his force. One day, he overheard one of his salesmen giving a rosy sales pitch to a prospective buyer regarding the city's future, and he commented, "They just can't lie about Lincoln Park, no matter what they say. This city has the best future of any town west of Detroit."

Maurice Levy died in 1949, but not before he made his mark on Lincoln Park. He was one of the charter members of Lincoln Park's first service organization, the Exchange Club. He also helped plan the first Lincoln Park Day celebrations in the 1920s. Lincoln Park Day became such a self-proclaimed holiday that even the city hall and most businesses closed for the day. Levy also branched out into construction and built the city's first library and post office at Fort Street and Russell. When Fort Street was widened beginning in 1926, Levy's office building was moved back twenty feet.

This image from 1921 is very revealing. The view is looking south on Fort Street toward State Street (Southfield Road). A nicer main street, downtown area was forming as the real estate boom was beginning to pick up steam. Notice the real estate advertising in the background. *Lincoln Park Historical Museum.*

This 1921 image provides a view looking north on Fort Street from State Street (Southfield Road). The busy street shows a growing, vibrant area with an interesting detail on the far right. The existence of a hardware and paint store indicates business and residential growth for the newly formed Village of Lincoln Park. *Lincoln Park Historical Museum.*

Top: Lincoln Park experienced a lot of construction in the 1920s. This image shows Fort Street heading north at Arlington Street. Everywhere in this picture there is a bustle of activity, businesses being constructed as well as houses. The smoke in the distance is from the Ford Rouge Plant three miles away. *Lincoln Park Historical Museum.*

Bottom: In 1921, M.R. Levy established a real estate office near the corner of Fort Street and Southfield Road. He played a huge role in the early development of Lincoln Park. His headquarters was the first modern brick building in the Village of Lincoln Park. *Lincoln Park Historical Museum.*

Other early realtors included Mark Goodell; B.A. Horger (who developed subdivisions near the central part of the village and donated space for the new school named for him in 1923); Houseman-Spitzley; Lincoln Park Realty (owned by the Keleman family); Frank Livernois; John O'Connor and Floyd Harrison; Silas Campau; George Shanley; and Arthur Weston. Some had local offices, while others were headquartered in offices in downtown Detroit. Realtor Arthur Zirkaloso, a war veteran who ran successfully for mayor in 1931, built his office at 3800 Fort Street near Riverbank Street; the small wooden frame building can still be seen there today.

As the development of various areas intensified and parcels were carved out for neighborhood and business use, one of the greatest needs was improvement of the roads. As mentioned previously, the area, up to the 1920s, primarily consisted of narrow, muddy wagon routes that became impassable after intense rain. The solution was to begin smoothing out and paving the dirt roads. It would be a local business that would play a major role in providing a solution. Michael and Sophia Sabadash and their family moved into the area in 1918 from Austria-Hungary. The family first settled in Pennsylvania and then moved to Michigan and settled on four acres along Pepper Road in Ecorse Township. Initially, a trucking and road building operation was established by Michael Sabadash. His operation grew into a large industrial concern. In time, his son Charles joined the business, and the company became known as Sabadash and Sabadash.

Road-paving projects in the 1920s called for cinders, available from chemical plants in Wyandotte. Trucks from Sabadash and Sabadash hauled the materials needed for surfacing many of the early roads that were a part of improving Fort Street, Dix Avenue, Southfield Road, Pepper Road (Outer Drive) and Telegraph Road. As the operation grew, the involvement of the company went beyond just transporting the cinders, as they acquired the equipment necessary to pave the roads as well. Sabadash and Sabadash was located at 1075 Pepper Road (Outer Drive). The historical record shows the company still operating into the 1970s, at which time the family moved out of Lincoln Park and the buildings were sold and torn down.

Another interesting real estate development within Lincoln Park as well as other growing communities was the construction of what became known as garage houses. By the mid-1920s, these structures had become much more commonplace than is known today. The idea behind this trend was that individuals would purchase a lot in a newly platted subdivision. Instead of building a larger house immediately, a smaller garage-sized house would be built with the intention of adding onto the original structure

Located at 1075 Pepper Road (Outer Drive), it was a local Lincoln Park firm, Sabadash and Sabadash, that played a major role in the improvement of area roads. Trucks from Sabadash and Sabadash hauled the materials needed for surfacing Fort Street, Dix Avenue, Southfield Road, Pepper Road and Telegraph Roads. In time, they acquired the equipment necessary to pave the roads as well. *Lincoln Park Historical Museum.*

Pictured is one of the "garage houses" built in Lincoln Park in the early 1900s. This particular example was owned by Henry and Jennie Rumsley. *Lincoln Park Historical Museum.*

More examples of garage houses that were built in the area. As Lincoln Park grew, the construction of these small houses allowed new residents to quickly move into an area that was seen as desirable. The owners intended to increase their living quarters in time, but in many cases and for a variety of reasons, that time never came. *Lincoln Park Historical Museum.*

when needed. However, after some time went by, many owners decided that the smaller structure was satisfactory, and further development was never attempted. Numerous garage houses can still be found in Lincoln Park today.

In terms of real estate used for business development within Lincoln Park, between the time Lincoln Park became a village and the year it became a city, several mom-and-pop businesses were established. Johnson's Store was an example of a general store that offered numerous staples to its customers. The role general stores played in the development of many towns and cities cannot be overstated. The goods and services they provided were absolutely vital to the survival of the community. Lincoln Park can be taken as a case study. In the early 1900s, there were few merchants in the area. A general store like Johnson's existed to provide a more convenient general variety of whatever locals needed.

The owner of a general store had to be prepared to stock anything, to sell items in and out of season and to keep on hand whatever might be

Shown here in 1923, Johnson's Store provided much-needed goods and services in a time of transition from a more rural area to existence as a village or town. *Lincoln Park Historical Museum.*

required by customers at any time during the year. Items like long underwear were available in the summer and plows in the winter. When watermelons were ready for sale, space would be made for them, and when they were gone, tomatoes or corn or some other crop or tool or medicine or cloth would be pulled out from under the counter and set in their place. Stores like Johnson's also provided services like banking and credit; shoe fitting; postal service; money orders; town telephone; town news center; community meetings; political rallies; evangelism; message sending; gun sales; whiskey sales; pharmacy; and a wide variety of products such as dairy, toys, clothing for all sizes and needs from denim to lace, flour, sledgehammers, ribbons, needles, mule harness, entire buggies including the whips, pencils, perfume and even once legal opium.

Smaller grocery stores or markets also had an important role to play. As the transition from a rural area to a suburban community began to happen, many residents no longer had access to a farm and traveling to a farmer's market might be miles away and less than convenient. The convenience of being able to visit a local establishment and stock up on necessary food-related items including various types of meat, was a huge advantage for any community. The Lincoln Park area has had several examples of this type of business over the years. As mentioned in the previous chapter,

Pictured are Fredrico and Winifred Angioletti, who built and managed Angiolet's Store at 1506 Lafayette Boulevard. They started the business in 1923 and lived above the establishment. *Lincoln Park Historical Museum.*

Toleikis Grocery was established before Lincoln Park was incorporated. In a later chapter, other well-known markets, Chiarelli's and Karol's, are discussed. Between the time of Lincoln Park's incorporation as a village and a city, Fredrico and Winifred Angioletti, natives of Italy, arrived in Lincoln Park and built a market on the southwest corner of Lafayette Boulevard and Russel Street in 1923. They named the business Angiolet's Store, and the couple lived above the establishment at 1506 Lafayette Boulevard. Their children were born above the store. According to their son Richard, "When I was fourteen, I would drive my dad to the farmer's market in Detroit so he could pick up the day's meat and produce. Dad never learned to drive, so he depended on us kids to get him around. Dad ran the store until the '50s, when supermarkets became popular." The building was torn down in 1988. Richard and his brother Joseph followed in their parents' footsteps in 1950 when they opened Stonefront Grocery at 2970 Fort Street. That establishment operated until 1970.

By the 1950s, general stores and smaller markets were starting to fade. Customers began to shift to the newly proliferating five-and-dime stores, chain grocery stores and big box offerings.

Angiolet's Store operated until the 1950s. The building was razed in 1988. *Lincoln Park Historical Museum.*

Pictured is the first hot dog stand in Lincoln Park. It began operating in 1923. The women on the porch are sisters-in-law Edna Quandt Wilber and Beth Wilber Miller, who managed the stand. *Lincoln Park Historical Museum.*

Mother's Restaurant was one of the early dining options in the city of Lincoln Park. This business was established the same year Lincoln Park was incorporated as a city, 1925. The menu consisted of soup and sandwiches. *Lincoln Park Historical Museum.*

Ready-made food offerings began to appear as well. Some of the first edible fare offered locally was what could best be characterized as bare bones and basic, but again, these establishments serviced and filled a developing need. An example of this was the first hot dog stand, set up in Lincoln Park in 1923. The hot dog stand was very near the Quandt Saloon on what is today Fort Street and Southfield Road. It was owned by the Quandt family and the Wilber family. Sisters-in-law Edna Quandt Wilber and Beth Wilber Miller managed the stand. It is unclear when the stand closed or what happened to the structure; however, when Fort Street was extended through to Champaign Road in 1926, it is probable that the building was razed due to the road construction and new development.

Another early dining option was Mother's Restaurant. The founding of Mother's will forever be connected to the incorporation of Lincoln Park as a city in 1925. Lincoln Parkers affectionately called the establishment—located on the corner of Fort Street and Warwick Avenue—the "pig stand." The menu consisted of soup and sandwiches. Owned and operated by Dorothy Crombie, Mary O'Connor and Nellie Etchell, it is unclear when Mother's Restaurant ceased operations and when the structure was torn down, but it is a classic example of the establishment of ready-made food options in the Lincoln Park area.

Chapter 4

PLACES TO EAT, DRINK AND ENJOY SOME RECREATION

While the building of a city certainly takes an enormous amount of work and dedication, the need to refresh one's body, soul and spirit is also called for in terms of a healthy and balanced human existence. To provide for these human needs and wants, Lincoln Park has offered numerous unique places over the years. Whether it was a place to grab a tasty meal or enjoy some drink and recreation, there have existed several locations worthy of discussion.

When it comes to entertainment venues throughout Lincoln Park's history, none is more iconic than the Park Theater. The Park Theater was born during the era of silent films. On August 15, 1925, the theater opened its doors for the first time and served Lincoln Park and the surrounding area for decades. The venue continues to live in the hearts of many area residents. The following piece, detailing the history of the Park Theater, was written by a Lincoln Park Historical Society member who worked there in the 1950s:

> *The Park Theatre was located at 1583 Fort Street, Lincoln Park, Michigan. It was built in 1925 and was able to accommodate 600 customers. The building was approximately 60 feet wide by 160 feet long. It was designed by C. Howard Crane* [1885–1952], *a well-known architect who designed close to 250 theatres around the country including 62 in the Detroit area. Orchestra Hall and The Olympia Stadium in Detroit were also designed by Crane. M.R. Levy constructed the Park Theatre. Silent movies were shown there in the early days. A piano was situated in front of the stage during*

the silent days. Silent movies began around 1894. The first "talkie" came out in 1927.

During the 1950s and 1960s, it was owned by Whisper & Wetsman. They owned numerous other movie theaters in the Detroit Metro area and in other parts of the country. The company was headquartered out of Birmingham, Michigan. By 1938, as movies with sound became more popular, the building was remodeled. Around this time, the front façade roof area was changed to add a different "Park" sign, and the marquee was changed from a rectangular shape to a larger one with angled sides. The new sign was larger and could hold 3 rows of clip-on lettering on each side as well as a short message on the front section. The newer marquee also had yellow light bulbs surrounding the lettering which sequenced in order which gave the appearance of movement. It was also an eye catcher for passing motorists. White light bulbs were installed on the underside of the marquee.

Air conditioning was added around the same time. It was a "swamp cooler" or evaporative cooler type that utilized water evaporation to produce chilled air. The air conditioning was a huge deal because it was not available for residential housing in those days. Many people came to the theatre to cool off during hot summer days and evenings.

However, one major drawback was that the law of physics caused cold air to drop down which meant that seats near the stage were often extremely cold since the floor descended toward the stage.

When the screen was replaced by a wider cinemascope type is unknown. In the beginning, theatres were able to continue using the 35mm format although it was vertically compressed and required a modification to the projector lens to "stretch" the image onto the screen. Later, some theatres switched to a 65/70 mm film format.

The Park Theatre received a second remodeling around 1960. It was minor but involved removing much of the beautiful 1930s style décor. The large, leafy wallpaper hanging in the lobby was removed and replaced with bland beige paint. The special mirrors were taken away, as was the scale, and the ticket stub box. A new stainless-steel box replaced the old one. A pop machine was added. New carpeting was also laid.

Retail space was available at both front corners, housing various establishments such as a barber shop, beauty salon, ice cream parlor, jewelry store, etc. They were approximately 15 by 15 feet square. A door to the small basement furnace room was located on the south wall of the lobby. Opposite this door on the north side was the stairwell going up to the

Here is the Park Theater as it looked when it was first built in 1925 by M.R. Levy. Silent movies were shown there for the first few years accompanied by a piano. Located at 1583 Fort Street, the venue provided entertainment and special experiences for five decades. *Lincoln Park Historical Museum.*

In 1936, the Park Theater was renovated and given a more modern façade. In the mid-1970s, patronage declined for numerous reasons, and the theater closed. The location unsuccessfully tried to operate as an adult entertainment venue. In 2009, the building was converted into lofts and retail space. *Lincoln Park Historical Museum.*

manager's office to the north and the Projection Room Booth to the south. At the very back of the building were separate rooms containing the ladder and letters for the marquee (north side) and another room (south side) for the air conditioning system. Access to both was through the outside doors only.

Before 1960, the lobby had a large oval mirror (approximately 3 feet wide by 4 feet tall) hanging on the walls on each side of the interior. A person could gaze into either mirror and see an infinite display of mirrors as the image reflected back and forth, each smaller than the last image. The ticket box was a small gutted out coffee grinder from the early days of the theater. It stood about 4 feet tall and was about 16 by 16 inches square. The top section was a ceramic "sided" funnel for stubs to drop down into a container below. There was about 12 inches of glass below it. The lower section was red painted wood with a door for removal of the spent ticket stubs. Ticket stubs were counted each night to match up with each day's sales to guard against money being embezzled. That beautiful ticket box was replaced by a larger stainless-steel box during the remodeling. The old scale which sat along the south wall of the lobby was also removed. The machine not only read a person's weight but also produced paper quotations for amusement.

A concessionary was located within the lobby and was operated by Mary "Ma" Muegge for many years through the 1940s, 1950s, and 1960s. The usual fare such as candy, popcorn, and drinks were available although drinks were initially not allowed beyond the lobby area. Later, around 1958, a pop dispenser was added in the lobby. Popcorn that was not sold one day would be saved and sold the next day. When the theater opened each day, Ma would begin to pop fresh popcorn but would then mix the freshly popped with the popcorn from the previous day. Later, when more popcorn was made, she would take a large piece of cardboard to the doors between the lobby and the seating area and begin fanning. The aroma of the fresh popcorn would waft into the seating area and soon, dozens of customers would come out wanting to purchase a box of popcorn.

Two sets of double doors separated the lobby from the seating area. Inside the theatre section was a half wall approximately 7 to 8 feet tall separating the entry area from the seating area. It had curtain covered windows above at about 4 feet high. During "standing room only" days, late arriving customers stood there while viewing the show through the windows. Many more sat in the aisles. That is until the city fire department banned such practice due to fire laws. Emergency double doors were located on both sides of the theatre near the front and the back of the seating area.

Two aisles ran from the back (lobby end) to the front (screen end) separating the seats into 3 sections. It is estimated that there were around 30 to 35 rows. The walls were narrower at the front by the width of about 4 seats on each side. The reason for this was to ensure the best view possible from any seat. Since the building was rectangular, the inner walls curved inward as one approached the stage area. Openings existed in those walls to allow for heat passage into the theatre from the water heating pipes. Ushers could walk into that hollow space to look out over the audience.

The heating for the building was provided by a coal furnace which utilized an auger to drive coal into the boiler. Heated water was pumped along both sides of the building. The furnace room was in the small basement on the south side of the lobby. Coal was loaded into a hopper via a small steel door along O'Conner Street. A large steel grating on the sidewalk provided open air access to the furnace room. The air conditioning unit was located in a separate room behind the screen on the south side of the building.

The theatre was regularly open on Saturdays and Sundays from 11:00 a.m. until around 1:00 p.m. when the last movie ended and on weekdays from around 6:00 p.m. to around 1:00 p.m. when the last movie ended. It was common to have two movies shown each day. One showing would be a recent release while the other one was often a B movie. On weekdays, the recent release would be shown first and last while the other movie was shown in between them. Upon opening each day, it was important for the ushers to slowly draw open the huge curtains covering the screen as the movie began. The projectionist dimmed the room lights at the same time. There was also a secret button above the water fountain near the men's room that was used to signal the projectionist to raise or lower the audio (one push meant raise and two pushes meant lower). The projectionist also had a window he could open to look out over the audience.

Cartoons and other short films were played between movies. An experience at the theater also included ongoing short movies such as Batman which usually ended each time as a "cliff hanger" where customers were lured back the following week to see if Batman and Robin would survive. Additionally, short newsreels were also played throughout the 1950s. It is important to note that televisions were not widespread until the early 1950s. This meant that if people wanted to see footage of various news articles including war related material, they could only see it at the theaters via the Warner-Path newsreels. The theater was used as a campaign headquarters to raise money for war bonds during World War II.

At opening time and closing time, side wall lighting was turned up to a high level for audience ingress and egress. During shows, these lights would be dimmed. Tiny lights shown [sic] *down on the aisles from the sides of seats every few rows during movie time. The walls and ceiling were quite decorative in the 1930s style.*

Early on, a carbon arc flame provided the bright lighting needed to project the film onto the screen. Each projector used two carbon rods, one positive and one negative about the size of a wooden pencil. They were ignited by low voltage, high amperage electricity. One of the carbon rods would burn four inches per reel, thus requiring frequent replacement during the show. Each movie reel held 20 minutes of 35mm film. Usually, 3 reels were contained in a metal carrying box. This meant that with two movies, cartoons, and newsreels, there could be 7 heavy containers to deliver upstairs to the projection booth. Each reel held 2,000 feet of film that ran at 24 frames per second. Two projectors were used during the shows. As one projector was about to reach its 20-minute run time, the second projector would be ready to switch on. The projectionist watched for a small symbol at the upper right section of the screen to know when to start the next projector and also synchronize the two films so that customers would not notice any breaks in the action. Sometimes the film would break or jam. Jams were as bad as breaks because the hot carbon arc would quickly burn through the film.

In either case, the projectionist would go into panic mode and quickly splice the broken ends together. Movies typically lasted from Sunday through Tuesday and from Wednesday through Saturday. After closing and late at night, a driver would come by, enter the theater to deliver the next set of movies and posters while picking up the previous sets to deliver to another theater or to be sent back to the movie companies. If the movie was hugely popular such as The Ten Commandments, it might remain at the theater for one or two weeks. Long movies often did not have a second movie accompanying it. One of the theater managers of note was Mr. Richmond. Mr. Richmond had a very long career at the Park Theater (1920s into the 1950s) and reportedly played the organ near the stage during the early silent film days. During the Christmas season of 1934, at the height of the depression, he issued free admission tickets to patrons who could not afford them.

By the mid-1970s, the theatre could no longer make a profit, and it closed down. There were a number of issues that brought about the downfall of the theater. Free parking between north and south bound Fort

Street had been banned by the state by 1960, so little parking was available. Also, television and home air conditioners were partly to blame for reduced attendance. The changing interests of the public and an increasing number of entertainment options also played a role. In 1980, the building was re-opened as an Adult Entertainment Show. It closed its doors in 2008, partly due to public pressure to have a more family-friendly venue located in the area. The Wayne Metropolitan Community Action Agency purchased it as part of an action settlement between the city and the Hustler Club and control was transferred to a non-profit organization.

The Downtown Development Authority and the Economic Development Corp donated $50,000 to convert the building into lofts and retail space. Reconstruction began in 2009. The old building was completely revamped except for the front section and outer side walls. The outer brick side walls were reinforced to accommodate windows and doors. The grand opening was held on January 15, 2015. Today, the structure is known as Lincoln Park Lofts. It holds 12 apartments and two retail spaces of 1200 sq. ft. each.

One additional note about the Park Theater. In later years, the venue shared its stage with live band performances from the modern rock-and-roll era of the 1960s. Locally formed garage bands often performed there, at a time when fame was just around the corner; the MC5, Bob Seger, Frigid Pink and many others would go on to concert tours and recording careers.

Another form of entertainment that became popular in the United States in the early to mid-twentieth century was bowling. It was an activity that could involve the whole family and one in which the skill level of all participants could include a wide range. During the Depression, there was a growing demand for inexpensive entertainment. Giuseppe "Joe Sr." and Natalina Clemente, who had immigrated to the United States from Italy just a few years earlier, settled in the recently incorporated city of Lincoln Park. Looking to meet this demand for entertainment during Prohibition, the couple initially opened a billiard hall at 2180 Fort Park Boulevard in 1930.

By 1932, most Americans were eager to end the experiment of Prohibition. A major movement was started to repeal the Eighteenth Amendment, and Michigan was the first state in the country to ratify the new Twenty-First Amendment, which effectively repealed Prohibition. Once this occurred, beer could be sold legally in Michigan. The Clementes were granted a beer license in 1933, and shortly afterward, Clemente's Bar was opened. Joe and Natalina had three children, and all of them would grow up to work in and

In 1946, the Clemente family opened a new location for their bar and restaurant. Located at 2230 Fort Street, the establishment was very successful, and in 1971, the building was renovated with a cedar-shingle roof and exterior stone wall. *Lincoln Park Historical Museum.*

operate the family business. Just prior to World War II, the name "Italian Village" was added to the marquee. When Italy joined the Axis powers during the World War II, City of Lincoln Park officials asked the family to change the name of the business.

When World War II ended, Clemente's moved its business to 2230 Fort Street and added a full-service restaurant and, shortly thereafter, a six-lane bowling alley. The unique variety of food, drink and entertainment provided at Clemente's served the Lincoln Park area for eighty years. The business closed in June 2010. The building was torn down within months of closing, and an Advance Auto Parts was built on the land where Clemente's stood.

Another bowling venue, the Fort Park Recreation Bowling Alley, was built in 1938 and located at 2055 Fort Park Boulevard. Constructed by Herman Quandt, the bowling alley initially was owned and operated by his daughter Frances James. The early days of bowling did not include automatic pin setters (machine). Manual pin setting meant that a person, often a teenager,

Bowling was a very popular pastime throughout the 1900s. Looking to capitalize on this form of entertainment, Clemente's added a six-lane bowling alley in 1948. *Lincoln Park Historical Museum.*

would jump from lane to lane and manually pick up the pins and place them back in their correct spot. Donald Wallace, who grew up in Lincoln Park in the 1930s and 1940s and wrote down his memories, worked at Fort Park Bowling Alley as a pin setter, and he related:

> *As an early teen, I spent many a weekend and nighttime hours setting pins in that great old smoke-filled place. It offered many Lincoln Park teenagers jobs when we were too young to work elsewhere. We were paid five cents a game. I once calculated how many tons I lifted during the four hours but can't remember the total now…I do know that the ball weighed at least fifteen pounds, and each pin weighed four or five pounds. On some nights you were given the chance to "jump alleys," which meant you set pins on both alleys, meaning double pay for double work. I quickly learned how to pick up as many as six pins with one stoop and learned how to pick up the heavy ball with a flick of my wrist and send it back on the ball return and quickly learned exactly how high I had to lift my feet so that the ball or pins*

wouldn't hit my legs. I remember after the league ended for the night, some of the bowlers would roll a quarter or a fifty-cent piece down the alley for a job well done by the thirteen-year-old kid.

There was a bar inside the bowling alley, and the smell of smoke was prevalent, as smoking was a common practice at that time. Due to the decline of league bowling as an activity, the facility closed in 2011. Presently, the structure is still standing.

When looking for a true old-school bar operating in Lincoln Park, area residents needed to look no farther than the Pioneer Inn. Located at 3406 Fort Street and Gregory, the building was constructed in 1945 and was the second bar owned by Earl Bernethy. Interestingly, the owner and operator made sure that his legacy would live on by engraving his name and the year his business was established above the door. Unfortunately, remodeling of the building has covered up the engraving. After it closed, Route 66, a diner,

Fort Park Bowling Alley was built in 1938 at 2055 Fort Park Boulevard. In the early years of the establishment, there were no automatic pin setters or ball returns. Individuals were hired as pin setters. Their job description included jumping from lane to lane, manually picking up pins, setting each on the proper spot and rolling the ball back to the bowler. *Lincoln Park Historical Museum.*

Pioneer's Inn was an old-school bar located at 3406 Fort Street. It was built in 1945 and first owned by Earl Bernethy. Today, the building houses a Mexican restaurant and bar. *Lincoln Park Historical Museum.*

The Old German Village Beer Hall was originally located at 1526 Fort Street. The bar featured hand-painted murals depicting scenes of German village life in the past. At the beginning of World War II, the name was changed to the Village Inn at the request of the city. *Lincoln Park Historical Museum.*

moved into the building and, later, an insurance agency. Today, the structure looks a bit different but is still standing and is home to a Mexican eatery.

Another drinking establishment that was well known in the early decades of Lincoln Park was the Old German Village Beer Hall. This was more than just a bar; it was a tribute to an entire culture. Opened in 1933 and originally located at 1528 Fort Street, the interior featured hand-painted murals depicting scenes of historical German life. The original owners of the business were William "Bud" Humphrey and his wife, Lucille, who lived in the second-floor apartment above the business. During World War II, because of Germany's involvement with the Axis powers, Lincoln Park city leaders asked Humphrey to change the name of the establishment, and the bar became known as the Village Inn. The business sponsored local amateur football teams that played across the street in a field next to the Park Theater. The Humphreys sold the business in the mid-1940s, and it continued to operate under various owners through the 1970s. For a while, the structure housed a chiropractic practice.

Chapter 5

PLACES TO LEARN

School days in most communities are associated with endearing memories that last a lifetime. The first classes to be held in what is today known as Lincoln Park took place in a private dwelling. Samuel LeBlanc, a pioneer settler in the area, allowed his home at Champaign Road and Fort Park Boulevard to be used for the purpose of education beginning in the 1850s. LeBlanc's daughter Florence LeBlanc Bodary related memories she heard from her father and also from her own experiences attending the first one-room school.

The first structure built strictly for education, according to Florence, was "a one-room school, called the Goodell School, built in the 1870s on a quarter-acre of land obtained from Toddy Beaufort at Fort Park Boulevard and Lincoln Street." The school was named for Cleophus Goodell, a descendant of one of the first English-speaking families in the area. When Florence attended classes there in the 1890s, the school board officers consisted of a who's who of area pioneer names: Thomas Goodell, director; Joseph Bondie, moderator; and August Keppen, treasurer. Florence, when interviewed about her school days, fondly remembered 1897, the year that "the school board purchased a big map on an easel, a globe of the world and a Webster's Dictionary." She also remembered the furnishings, which included a stove, a supply of wood, a water pail and dipper, a broom, six erasers and two boxes of chalk.

Around the turn of the century, the schoolhouse was moved to Champaign Road and placed on land purchased from Joseph Bondie. It was around this time that the students were divided into grades. In terms of the day-to-day structure of learning and how students progressed through to graduation, Florence's memories provide a picture that has been lost to time:

> *Pupils worked up through the fifth reader, then studied history. When they passed their history examination, their education was complete. Later, pupils used the Harper Reader, Barnes' Brief History of the United States, and the textbooks on geography, arithmetic, spelling, grammar and physiology. The library was actually in the Goodell home. For penmanship we had our copy book. For lessons and homework, we used slates or wrapping paper.*
>
> *We also used the H.R. Patengill Knapsack song book. When Mr. Turk, our Civil War veteran teacher, led us in "Marching Through Georgia," we had to sing with all our might and main. But when we sang, "Tenting Tonight on the Old Campground," we sang soft and low.*
>
> *I remember one year we celebrated Arbor Day by planting four trees in the school yard, naming them Goodell, Bondie, Keppen and Turk for our teacher and school officials. Our first flag was purchased with pennies collected from the children by the teacher. Using a hammer and jackknife, he managed to put up a flagpole on the front of the school. The was no belfry, and we used only a handbell to call students into school. That flag on the schoolhouse may have been the first flag to be flown in Lincoln Park.*
>
> *Speaking of hard-working, underpaid teachers of today, teachers then taught pupils ranging in age from 4 to 18 years in one room. The men teachers, hired in the winter months, had to plow through snow to get to school, then light the fire in the wood stove, clean up the building, and teach all the different age groups for the fabulous sum of about $28 per month. For the spring term, we had a woman teacher, who was "luckier" because of the milder weather. She only had to wade ankle deep in water, mud and clay, cross overflowing ditches on a wood plank, do the janitor work at the school, and teach German and French for pupils who could not understand English. She did all of this for about $20 a month. If she didn't live close by, she even had to pay for board and lodging.*
>
> *I never heard any of them complain, and on the last day of school they would have us recite poems, conduct spelling bees and read essays for our parents and school officers who always came to the last session. Then the teacher would usually give each pupil a picture for remembrance. Older children seldom started school until late fall and usually stopped attending classes early in the spring. The older girls of the family had to help with housework and caring for the babies, while the boys had to help with woodcutting and harvesting.*

Joseph LeBlanc, a son of Samuel LeBlanc, also recorded his memories of his school days attending the same school. Mr. Turk, mentioned in the previous memory, made a great impression on his students, and again, this speaks to a time and a way of educating that is now long past and lost to history:

> *The first teacher on the new site was Oscar J. Turk, an old Civil War veteran who had an all-time average of 5 broken rulers per day and a double pointed stick that he could shoot across the room with great dexterity if the occasion demanded. In other words, a teacher of the old school, a hard task master. By that I mean hard on the kids. The kids toted revolvers in those days, and I don't mean wooden ones. They even vaccinated in those days, as the school was used for this purpose one time.*

This vaccine Joseph refers to would have been protection against smallpox infection. The first smallpox vaccine was created in 1796, and in the mid-1800s, states began to require that children receive the vaccine to prevent the spread of smallpox in schools.

This is the second school building named for Cleophus Goodell. Built in 1918 at the corner of Fort Street and Champaign Road, this structure contained four classrooms. *Lincoln Park Historical Museum.*

Over time, a gymnasium and an auditorium were added onto Goodell School. The school served the community until, due to declining enrollment, it closed in 1971. The building was razed in 1974. *Lincoln Park Historical Museum.*

In 1918–19, the old wood-frame structure was replaced with a new brick building on the corner of Fort Street and Champaign Road. The initial schoolhouse contained four classrooms with a gymnasium. An auditorium was added a few years later. At the time of its construction, this version of the Goodell School was one of the most modern buildings in the Downriver area. The school was built just a few years before the incorporation of the city of Lincoln Park. H.W. Hicks was the first principal, and he had a staff of five teachers. In addition to serving as a place for students to be educated, the building also became the headquarters for the board of education and housed the central offices. After serving the community for over fifty years, the school was forced to close in 1971 due to declining enrollment. The building was razed in 1974, and the school bell was donated to the Lincoln Park Historical Museum.

The original plans for the Goodell School bell called for it to be housed in a scaled-down version of the school building. However, when the museum moved into the former United States Post Office, there was a change in plans. Joseph P. Griggs drew up plans for a four-sided tower where the bell would be mounted on top inside of a pointed shingle roof with a weathervane included. The structure was built using bricks from the school and from other Lincoln Park schools, including Raupp, Horger and the first High School. The Goodell Tower Bell was dedicated on October 17, 1999, and a time capsule was sealed on January 1, 2000. Every New Year's Eve, the bell of the Goodell School is rung at midnight to welcome in the New Year.

Another historic school worthy of discussion was the Strowig School. Frederick Strowig was a German immigrant and farmer who settled in the area. In 1850, he gave a tract of land to Ecorse Township officials for the express purpose of building a school on the property. A wooden frame structure was built on Pepper Road (Outer Drive) and served the area for many years. Oral histories relate stories of students trudging up a dusty road to get to the school in order to learn English. Many of those early residents spoke German and French.

In 1921, the year Lincoln Park became a village, the building was moved from Pepper Road to Fort Street in what today is southwest Detroit. In

The original Strowig School was named for Frederick Strowig, a German immigrant who settled in the area. He donated a tract of land for the purpose of having a school built. A wood-frame, one-room schoolhouse was erected on Pepper Road (Outer Drive). The building was moved to Southwest Detroit in 1921 to make room for a larger brick structure. *Lincoln Park Historical Museum.*

In 1921, this more modern Strowig School was built to replace the original one-room wooden schoolhouse. This 1922 image shows the students, faculty and Mr. Scott, the principal, ready to start a new school year. The building had a short life because Wayne County purchased the school in 1926 and tore it down in order to widen Fort Street. *Lincoln Park Historical Museum.*

its new location, this building served as a church, candy store, ice cream parlor and many other enterprises. There were several discussions by city officials over the years about bringing the structure back to Lincoln Park to serve as a museum, but that plan never materialized. In 1957, the building was razed.

The Strowig name lived on, however, in the form of a new brick structure erected on the Pepper Road site in 1921. It was more of a modern building and contained four classrooms. One of the teachers present at the dedication of this new building was not even eighteen years old yet. His name was Arnold Gregory, and he was just seventeen in 1921 and had to wait until he turned 18 on August 5, 1921, before signing his teaching contract at Strowig School. Gregory would serve the Lincoln Park schools, including over twenty years as high school principal, until his retirement in 1967. He then served as a city councilman for several terms. Arnold Gregory, for whom Gregory Park is named, died in 1981 at age seventy-eight. He served the community as a public servant for over fifty years. As fate would have it though, Strowig School existed for only five years. When Fort Street was converted into a "superhighway," the structure was demolished in 1927.

As Lincoln Park grew, schools were constructed in rapid succession. In less than nine years, Raupp, Horger, Lafayette and Hoover grade schools were

Construction began on William Raupp School in 1921. The school, located at 1351 Ethel Street, opened in 1924. The dedication of the school attracted a large crowd, with the school's namesake making a speech and presenting the school with a large flag. *Lincoln Park Historical Museum.*

constructed, and a high school was added to the school system. Prior to this addition, Lincoln Park residents had to attend high school classes at either River Rouge or Wyandotte high schools.

Construction began on the William Raupp School in 1921, and the doors opened in January 1924. The school was located at 1351 Ethel Street. Arnold Gregory, mentioned previously, transferred from the Strowig School and became the principal at Raupp School. The dedication of the school attracted over eight hundred people. Dedication festivities included music and numerous speeches. One of the commentators, Assistant School Commissioner Fred Fischer, stated in his speech that "one room schoolhouses were being discontinued, and larger standard schools (like Raupp) were taking their place."

William Raupp, the school's namesake, was also present at the school's dedication. He presented the school with a large flag. At the time, he was serving as president of the Village of Lincoln Park. Raupp had lived through and experienced a tremendous amount of history and change in the area when he gave this dedication speech. His words reveal much about the evolution of the area up to this point in time:

> *It is usually customary for a speaker to talk about someone else. However, I am going to change that custom a little and try and say a few words about myself. As a usual thing, buildings, monuments, books, etc. are dedicated to some dead person, to someone that has been prominent in the community or has died in its service. After careful consideration, I have come to one conclusion only and that conclusion seems to be a case of "Die to Win" so to speak.*
>
> *I well remember forty years back when all of the territory through here was generally farmland and when the school enrollment was about thirty in number. At that time, we knew the neighbors for miles around, of which these were the most prominent: The Abens; Quandts; Schonfelds; McQuades and the Riopelles.*
>
> *Time flew swiftly by until today we find ourselves living in a village of nearly eight thousand population. Fifteen years ago last July, the school district elected me as treasurer. I have served the people by holding this office ever since. In the records I notice that there has been a gradual increase in the school census, year by year, until the time came three years ago when the school facilities became inadequate for the increased number of scholars. To take care of this situation we voted to build the new Strowig School. It seems however that we miscalculated the speed with which the village would grow. We discovered last fall that we were in the same difficulty as we were in three years ago. Consequently, it was necessary to construct this building. We have patiently waited for its completion until tonight we find ourselves gathered together for its dedication. As a token of remembrance and to show my appreciation for the honor extended me I most gratefully present this flag to the school.*

The Raupp School organized the first Lincoln Park Parent Teacher Association (PTA). The school served the community well until 1999, when it was torn down and replaced by a new elementary school building that still bears the name Raupp.

Horger School, named for the man who created the Horger subdivision, was erected in 1922. B.W. Horger donated the land for the school with the understanding that the school built there would bear his name. The first principal was Lyman Galloway. The building served the community for over seventy years and was torn down in 1999.

The 1920s were a busy decade for building schools in the newly formed Lincoln Park. In 1926, another educational facility was constructed at 1360 Lafayette Boulevard. Known as Lafayette School, the second floor was used

Horger School, named after B.W. Horger, was built in 1922. Horger, who was known in the area as the man who had platted the Horger subdivision, donated the land for the building of the school. The school is shown here as it looked in 1950. *Lincoln Park Historical Museum.*

for high school classes from 1928 to 1933. A new one-story school was built at the same location in 1997, and the original Lafayette School building was torn down in 1998.

As the Ford Rouge Plant continued to attract people to the area, and specifically Lincoln Park because of its proximity to the plant, the population increased from 250 in 1921 to over 12,000 in 1930. With the tremendous influx of new students and the need for new spaces to educate them, two new schools were constructed in 1930. The Hoover School was located at 3750 Howard Street and was named for President Herbert Hoover. The text printed on the dedication program tells why he was given this honor:

> *The educational philosophy of Herbert Hoover is in accord with the thinking of the leading educators of the country who are urging the exchange of new schools for old, of useful knowledge for worn out curriculums, of freedom from bondage, of joy for drudgery, and of useful education for all the children of all the people. Few men in America have done as much for children as Mr. Hoover and few understand them and their needs in scientific, social, and national aspects, as does our new president.*

In 1926, Lafayette School was completed, located at 1360 Lafayette Boulevard. High school classes were held in this structure in 1928 and 1929. A new one-story school was built on the site in 1998, and this building was razed the same year. *Lincoln Park Historical Museum.*

A bond issue in 1928 raised funds to construct Hoover School. Located at 3750 Howard Street, the school was named after President Herbert Hoover. The structure was halfway completed when the stock market crashed in October 1929. *Lincoln Park Historical Museum.*

Hoover School was in the middle of construction during the last week of October 1929 when the stock market crashed and sent the United States reeling into a decade-long depression. This event, however, did not keep the school from opening on time in 1930 with an enrollment of 235 grade school students. The school's first principal, Howard Derr, served in that capacity from 1930 until his retirement in 1966. A new wing was added to the building in the 1950s.

A Lincoln Park Historical Society member, Doris (Bitzer) Blessing, attended Hoover School from 1938 to 1944. Doris recalls the most significant memory of her Hoover years occurred on D-Day, June 6, 1944. That day, her teacher, Mrs. Lina Compton, was visibly upset and crying. The class learned that her husband was in the wave of soldiers involved in the invasion of Nazi-occupied France. In 2020, the ninety-year-old structure was razed to make room for a new Hoover School. The north wing, which had been added in the 1950s, was retained, and the original stone archway of the main entrance was incorporated into the new structure.

Huff Junior High School was also built in 1930 and originally served as Lincoln Park High School from 1933 until 1959. Named for Leo W. Huff, the first superintendent of schools in Lincoln Park, the high school was the first Michigan high school to be recognized by the University of Michigan before being accredited by the North Central Association. Huff joined the school system in 1928 and provided leadership during those early growth years. He was also instrumental in forming the school district's PTA Council in 1928. In 1956, Huff passed away, and the PTA established a memorial scholarship fund in his name. The scholarship continues to the present day. The building served as a junior high school for the rest of its existence from 1960 until it was razed in 1981 due to declining enrollment.

By the 1950s, Lincoln Park's population had increased to over forty thousand people, and with many new families settling in the city, there was a need for another elementary school. So, in 1951, the Richard LeBlanc School was constructed at 3804 Hazel Street. The school was named for Richard "Uncle Dick" LeBlanc, a descendant of a pioneer family and, at the time, the oldest living resident in Lincoln Park. Today, the building no longer operates as an elementary school but has transitioned into a facility used by Blessed Hope Church.

With the area still needing classroom space, in 1952, the May V. Smith Elementary School was erected at 1650 Champaign Road. The school began operations with an enrollment of 330 students. Over time, the

Top: What became known as Huff Junior High was originally Lincoln Park High School. The building served as a high school from 1933 until 1959. The school was named after Leo W. Huff, the first superintendent of schools in Lincoln Park. *Lincoln Park Historical Museum.*

Bottom: LeBlanc School was named after Richard "Uncle Dick" LeBlanc, who was the oldest resident living in Lincoln Park at the time of the school's construction. Built in 1951 at 3804 Hazel Street, today it is no longer an elementary school but is used by Blessed Hope Church. *Lincoln Park Historical Museum.*

Top: Built in 1952 at 1650 Champaign Road, this building was named after May V. Smith, an early resident of the area. After classes were discontinued, the structure became offices for the Lincoln Park Board of Education. *Lincoln Park Historical Museum.*

Bottom: Hamilton School was built in 1955 at 1590 Goddard Road. The school's namesake, George R. Hamilton, served on the first village school board. The school closed in 1975, and the building is now used for Montessori Child Development classes. *Lincoln Park Historical Museum.*

Erected in 1959, this school was named after Winfred S. Crowley, a local realtor who served on the school board from 1927 until 1967. The school closed in 1971 and is currently being used for a pre-K readiness program. *Lincoln Park Historical Museum.*

school transitioned to providing services to physically disabled and mentally impaired students. The school's namesake, May Smith, was an early resident in the area and went on to serve the community as PTA Council president and held a seat on the school board from 1927 until her death in 1947. Today, the building is no longer a school but is used for offices of the board of education.

As the decade of the 1950s continued to be one of growth, another school building was constructed in 1955. Hamilton School was named in honor of George R. Hamilton, who served on the first village school board. The school had a relatively short run in terms of serving as an elementary school. The school closed in 1975, and the building is now used for Montessori Child Development classes.

Just as the decade was coming to a close, another educational project was completed. The Winfred S. Crowley Elementary School was built in 1959. Named for a local realtor who served on the school board from 1927 until 1967, this was another facility that had a relatively brief existence as a public school. The school closed in 1971 and is currently being used for programming called the Great Start Readiness Program.

Chapter 6

PLACES TO WORSHIP

Another aspect of community life that was extremely important to the early pioneers and throughout the early development of Lincoln Park was the founding of churches. While there were churches established in the area prior to the formation of Lincoln Park, using the village incorporation year of 1921 provides a clear starting date for discussion. Many of the first organized churches were established in the 1920s.

The earliest religious body established in Lincoln Park was the First United Methodist Church. The organization was founded in 1921, the same year that Lincoln Park was incorporated as a village. Three different Methodist groups had been meeting in the area prior to this event, and the decision was made to join forces. To make this conglomeration happen, the interested parties obtained $800 from the Methodist Home Missions Board, and contributions were made by the Fort Street Methodist Church of Detroit as well as the future congregants. The money was used to purchase land that would be used for the building of a church.

A building was constructed on Victoria Street near Southfield Road. Once the foundation and subflooring were installed, chairs were borrowed from neighbors and the first service was held. The first pastor was Dr. M.S. Rice, a preacher who was widely known in the area. Over the first couple of years of its existence, the church held a membership drive, and the number of attending members soared from 26 to 115. It was not long before the leadership and members felt they had outgrown the initial building, and in 1925, it was sold to the First Baptist Church. Services were held in the Raupp School until a larger church building was erected at Fort Park Boulevard and

The first established religious body in Lincoln Park became official in 1921. The congregation of First Methodist Church built this wood structure on Victoria Avenue near Southfield Road. Over the years, this building became home to numerous congregations and earned the nickname "Lincoln Park's Cradle of Religion." *Lincoln Park Historical Museum.*

Anne Street. A large church bell was presented to the church by a group of Detroit-area businessmen and was part of the dedication.

The original building was used by several other congregations over the next several decades, including, as mentioned previously, the First Baptist Church, the Bethany United Methodist Church and the First Southern Baptist Church. Because the building served as a home for four different congregations, it earned a nickname: "Lincoln Park's Cradle of Religion." In 1962, the structure was torn down to make way for an urban renewal program. The First United Methodist congregation continued at their new location until 2024. The building at 1734 Fort Park Boulevard is presently for sale.

Two other Methodist churches have operated in Lincoln Park. The Free Methodist Church was established in 1927. A building was constructed at 2069 Chandler Street. It was transformed into Lighthouse Free Methodist Ministries, but that organization has not been active since 2019, and the building has been abandoned since that time.

The Dix United Methodist Church was founded in June 1923. Initial meetings took place in a home on Hanford Street in the form of Sunday

Built in 1925, the First Methodist Church congregation moved here after experiencing tremendous growth, and the church became known as the First United Methodist Church. The building, located at Fort Park Boulevard and Anne Street, continued at this location until 2024. The building is presently for sale. *Lincoln Park Historical Museum.*

The Free Methodist Church was established at this building at 2069 Chandler in 1927. The building currently is unoccupied. *Lincoln Park Historical Museum.*

school classes. When the weather was mild, the first congregation even met in a nearby wooded area. In 1924, B.A. Horger gifted two lots to the church to be used for the purposes of a meeting place. Initially, a basement was constructed on what is today known as Horger Street near Dix Avenue. Two years later, the upper portion of the building was completed. A new sanctuary was constructed in 1964. In 1966, the congregation from Fort Street Methodist Church merged with the Lincoln Park congregation. The building at 1911 Horger Street was destroyed by fire in 1973, and a new edifice was erected on the same site. This building served the congregation until operating the church was no longer viable due to decreased membership. The church closed in 2013. Worldwide Prophetic Kingdom Ministries presently occupy the building.

It should be noted that the Free Methodist Church had split off from the Methodist Episcopal Church in 1860. What separates the United Methodist Church from the Free Methodist Church is an interesting study. The Methodist Church was founded by John and Charles Wesley, who believed in methodical study of scripture and living a holy life. Because of this, there were those who mocked them by calling their approach "methodical," which led to the reference "methodists." In 1784, the Methodist Episcopal Church was born. The new church grew rapidly, and many came to the United States to spread the movement. Circuit riders were employed to travel to every corner until it was said there was "scarcely any village in the

Dix United Methodist Church was founded in 1923. The congregation met where they could until this structure was built on Horger Street near Dix Avenue. *Lincoln Park Historical Museum.*

United States without a Methodist presence." Over the years, there were many divisions and mergers about numerous issues. In 1844, the Methodist Episcopal Church split because of tensions over slavery. By then, the Methodist Church had become the largest Protestant denomination in the United States, and it would not be long until "Methodism" had traveled to what would become Lincoln Park.

The Free Methodist Church was birthed in 1860 when it was decided that they could no longer serve in harmony with the practices of the Methodist Episcopal Church. With the Civil War about to break out, those who became Free Methodists decided they could not support slaveholding, rent seats in the church, withhold women from full service in the church and quench the movement of the Holy Spirit in public worship. Therefore, this new branch of methodism was about promoting freedom for all people.

Roman Catholicism also made its way to the area. The diocese of Detroit was established by Pope Gregory XVI in 1833, more than one hundred years after French settlers built the first Catholic church during the founding of Detroit. At the time, the diocese included all of Michigan, Wisconsin, Minnesota and portions of the Dakotas, east of the Mississippi River. The diocese predates even the state of Michigan, which did not join the United States until 1837. At that time, the boundaries of the diocese were changed to fit into Michigan's newly established borders.

Saint Anne de Detroit Church was the first church built by settlers in the area in 1701. The church served as the diocese's first cathedral from 1833 to 1848. In 1937, Detroit was elevated to an archdiocese. In the following decades, the region's population grew steadily, which required the expansion of many parishes. By 1869, there were eighty-four churches in the area and sixty Catholic schools, and the Catholic population had expanded to 116,000.

The first Catholic church in Lincoln Park was founded in 1923. St. Henry Catholic Church initially met in a small frame building located at Fort Park Boulevard and Council Street with twenty-five families on the church roll. The church was named after St. Henry of Bavaria, a prominent fourteenth-century churchman. The church had astronomical growth in those early years, and by 1924, the membership had grown to over three hundred families. A two-story structure was built as temporary housing, with the first floor consisting of a parish hall, bowling alley and kitchen. The second floor could seat up to eight hundred people.

In 1928, a larger Gothic-style church was constructed along with the first parochial school in Lincoln Park. A more contemporary structure and an

Founded in 1923, the first Catholic church in Lincoln Park was known as St. Henry's. This two-story church had a parish hall, bowling alley and kitchen on the first floor. *Lincoln Park Historical Museum.*

even larger school were erected and dedicated in 1964. The last mass was held on March 2, 2014. The church closed due to declining attendance and lack of funds. On the last day of operation, anything of significance was carried out and relocated to Christ the Good Shepherd Catholic Church on Riverbank Street in Lincoln Park. Many former parishioners attended the final mass to say goodbye to an institution that had served the community for ninety-one years.

The building that stands at 1362 Chandler Avenue has served as shelter for numerous congregations throughout its history. From a Lutheran church to Greek Orthodox to Hungarian Baptist, the structure has been well used for almost ninety years now. The building was built in 1936 by Calvary Lutheran Church to be their new home. Calvary Lutheran was founded in the fall of 1923 by the Reverend Walter O. Kleinhans, who began the work as a mission project. Lutheranism was founded in the early sixteenth century when a German monk, Martin Luther, protested the Roman Catholic Church's practice of selling indulgences as part of the penance, or punishment, for those who sinned against church teachings. Luther believed that the church should reposition Christ as the center of

Membership at St. Henry's Catholic Church grew so rapidly that in 1928, a larger Gothic-style church was built at 1358 Council Avenue. Then in 1964, a contemporary church building, shown here, was built on the same site. *Lincoln Park Historical Museum.*

Christian worship, and he objected to the governance of the Catholic Church, as well as its treatment of communion and plan for salvation. Luther's central doctrine was "Justification through Faith," the belief that salvation can be attained only by faith in the grace of God and not by the performance of good works.

Lutherans arrived on the shores of America as early as 1742. The first official Lutheran church in Michigan was established in Ann Arbor in 1833. Three years later, Lutheran churches were founded in Detroit and a host of other towns in the area. A Lutheran congregation has existed in Lincoln Park since 1923. Calvary's first building was located on the corner of Cicotte Avenue and Chandler Street. Property was purchased and ground broken for a bungalow chapel. Christian day school classes began in the bungalow chapel. A two-room school was erected in late 1925. A church building was completed and dedicated at the end of 1926. As the congregation grew, a move was necessitated. A new site was acquired at the corner of Pagel and Electric Avenues in early 1955. The cornerstone of the new church was laid in April 1956, with the completed building dedicated in May 1957. Calvary celebrated its 100th anniversary in 2024.

In 1956, St. George Greek Orthodox Church purchased the Chandler Avenue building when the structure they had been meeting in was destroyed by a tornado. The Greek Orthodox Church claims to have been founded by Jesus Christ himself and states that the church was guided by the apostles, including Saint Paul, who visited many Greek cities and was strengthened by martyrs, saints and the Church Fathers. This church is maintained and propagated by believers in the modern world. The Greek Orthodox Church holds many of the same beliefs as the Catholic Church but practices in different ways. The two would agree on the importance of scripture and tradition and views on the Eucharist but disagree as to which traditions to honor. For example, the Greek Orthodox Church does not have a pope, but it does have its own ruling body.

Detroit saw a large increase of immigrants from Greece in the late nineteenth century, many fleeing economic woes that followed the country's war for independence. Many settled in the area known today as Greektown. With the growing number of Greek immigrants in Detroit, the State of Michigan issued a charter for establishment of a Greek Orthodox Church on March 25, 1910. This was the first Greek Orthodox church in the state of Michigan. St. George's community traces its beginnings to the 1930s, when seven families established a church in Lincoln Park. In 1945, the cornerstone for a church building was laid on Porter and Garfield Streets. With thirty-five families, the parish was chartered in 1951. Five years later, the congregation transitioned to the Chandler Avenue location. The St. George congregation worshiped there until the mid-1970s, when, due to tremendous growth, they relocated to Southgate. Not long after, the First Hungarian Baptist Church purchased the building in 1978.

The Hungarian Baptist mission in the area was founded in 1908. The first meeting took place in a house on Medina Street. The First Baptist Church was built in 1913 on Thaddeus Street. In 1931, the congregation at Highland Park was merged with that of First Baptist Church; however, the church on Thaddeus Street was too small, so a new church building was purchased on Vanderbilt Street. Services were held in that building for the next forty-eight years. In 1976, when Pastor András Herjeczki became the new leader, the congregation sold the church building. Less than two years later, the structure located at 1362 Chandler Street became their home, and it has remained so to the present.

In the early 1930s, a number of families moved into the area who shared specific religious beliefs connected with the Church of God denomination located out of Anderson, Indiana. This movement first appeared in the

Top: This building at Cicotte and Chandler Streets was completed in 1936 by the congregation of Calvary Lutheran. It has been home to several kinds of churches since and is presently occupied by First Hungarian Baptist Church. *Lincoln Park Historical Museum.*

Bottom: The Lincoln Park Church of God, established in 1937, moved into this building in 1944. Located at 888 Southfield Road, the building is currently not in use. *Lincoln Park Historical Museum.*

1880s during the broader American Holiness Revival. The pioneers of the Church of God hoped to restore a more biblical understanding and practice of what it meant to be the church. The core belief of the Church of God can be summed up by the following statement: The Bible is our rule of faith and Christ alone is Lord. The principle distinctive of the church as a Pentecostal organization is its belief in speaking with other tongues, as the Spirit gives the utterance, and that this is the initial evidence of the baptism in the Holy Spirit.

With the group wanting to form a congregation in Lincoln Park, the idea of growing a church took root in a house in 1937. In the fall of that year, the group rented a building on Southfield Road, and the Lincoln Park Church of God was officially founded. In 1943, the members moved to a rented building on Fort Street, and at that time, four lots were purchased, with plans for constructing a church in the future. Construction began in 1944 on a sanctuary located at 888 Southfield Road with the pastor, Lester Schrock, serving as the supervisor of the project and helping with the physical labor as well. In the 1950s, a Christian education wing was added along with a Sunday school program. Under the leadership of James Childs, who served the church from 1967 until 1981, the congregation became more involved in missions' outreach both locally and around the world. Presently, the church has ceased operations, and the building is currently not in use.

Chapter 7

PLACES TO BUY GOODS AND SERVICES

As any community grows, there is also an increasing need for individuals to start businesses that will provide goods and services to the residents of the area. The beginnings of a business district, as mentioned earlier in this publication, had its initial roots at Fort Street and St. Cosme Line (Southfield Road). The first businesses to crop up near this corner included a store operated by Noah LeBlanc and a grocery market established by Herman Quandt. Henry Ford's five-dollar-a-day wage and the building of the nearby Ford Rouge Plant brought such a rapid increase in population. This growth meant there was suddenly an intense need for additional providers of goods and services.

After the initial development of Quandt's Corners near what is presently Southfield Road and Fort Street, some of the earliest and longest-running businesses in the area were founded around the time Lincoln Park became a city. In fact, in 1925, the year the city of Lincoln Park was incorporated, Chiarelli's Market was founded by Ercole "Charlie" Chiarelli and Romeo Leone. Charlie came to the Detroit area and was initially employed by Dodge as a machinist. When he severed two fingers on the job, he was given a $500 settlement, which he used to start a market business. The original location of the business was at 2116 Fort Park Boulevard. In 1928, the market was moved across the street to 2210 Fort Park Boulevard. The first building, which was owned at the time by the Clemente family, became Clemente's Bar. It was around this time that Charlie met a recent arrival from Italy, Clara DeSanto. Charlie and Clara married in 1928. The family lived above their business, and two sons, Frank and Al, were born upstairs.

Numerous businesses have occupied the building at the corner of Fort Park and Garfield. Pictured is the interior when it was Chiarelli's Market, founded in 1925. *Lincoln Park Historical Museum.*

In 1935, Leone was bought out. Chiarelli's Market thrived for years. Frank and Al eventually took over ownership, and the store continued to be successful. Even as chain stores and larger supermarkets moved in, the customer base of this local market remained loyal. The reason, according to Frank, was a continued commitment to quality: "They were writing us off for years because we were a small store, but every time a chain came into our area, our business got better." Frank also believes that knowing what the customers want is a key component: "You have to analyze the customers' needs, you have to bring them into focus." At its peak, Chiarelli's served more than six thousand customers a week. The operation employed forty-four people and featured a delicatessen, bakery and butcher shop.

What Chiarelli's became most known for was the meat department, which at one time generated 40 percent of sales. Rather than buy precut beef, they ordered quartered steers from a Colorado slaughterhouse and employed three full-time meat cutters. Operating this way allowed the meat to properly age, which meant it was tastier and more tender. The owners considered moving several times, but the expense and losing the quaintness of the old-school atmosphere always kept that from happening. While

Charlie Chiarelli came to the United States from Italy. Chiarelli's Market became one of the most popular markets in the area. It remained in business for over eighty years. *Lincoln Park Historical Museum.*

people crave newer and more amenities, the Chiarellis always believed that their customers would miss the old store with its narrow aisles, tin ceiling and the fragrance of freshly baked bread. In the 1990s, Al's sons took over the management of the market. In 2008, after being in operation for over eighty years, Chiarelli's Market closed its doors for the last time. Los Arcos Market, a Mexican grocery store, complete with a meat counter and deli, has taken up residence in the structure.

Joseph and Ruth Blumrosen started what they called an economy store in 1925. The store was located at 1184 Fort Street on the corner of Fort Street and College Street. At the time, their shop would have been categorized as a dry goods store. Dry goods stores were popular around the turn of the twentieth century and sold products such as textiles, ready-to-wear clothing, toiletries and grocery items (such as tobacco, sugar, flour and coffee) that did not contain liquid. Both Joseph and Ruth believed deeply in community involvement, and they were members of and contributors to many Lincoln Park organizations. Joseph played a huge role in helping Lincoln Park build its own library. Ruth was a charter member of the Lincoln Park Women's Club and an integral member of the garden division. The landscaping

Joseph and Ruth Blumrosen started a dry goods store in 1925. It was located at 1184 Fort Street. The building is still standing but is currently vacant. *Lincoln Park Historical Museum.*

around their house looked like a nursery and included a rock garden, over five hundred rosebushes and close to two thousand tulips. When the Economy Store closed is unclear. The building is presently vacant.

Another market, Karol's Grocery, opened not long after Chiarelli's. Michael and Edna Karol opened their first store at 2205 Fort Street in 1929. A second store was established next door at 2215 Fort Street. Michael believed in good old-fashioned customer service. Born in Austria-Hungary, he opened a general store in Oklahoma when he first came to the United States. Making his way to Michigan, he operated his business based on the following motto: "Price is soon forgotten, but the memory of good will, honesty and quality last forever." A main feature inside the store was a soda bar against the wall. The first location served as a housing for many other businesses through the years, including Lincoln Park Groceries and Meats, Sager Photographic Studio, Scheidel & Kolton Appliance and Busen Appliance. Today, the structure is used by La Pinata Dulceria, a quaint and charming candy store specializing in traditional Mexican sweets and treats.

This structure served as many businesses through the years: Lincoln Park Groceries and Meats, Sager Photographic Studio, Scheidel & Kolton Appliance and Busen Appliance. Today, the structure houses La Pinata Dulceria, a Mexican candy store. *Lincoln Park Historical Museum.*

Donald W. Wallace, in his book *Growing Up in Simpler Times*, relates stories about growing up in Lincoln Park in the 1930s and 1940s and, specifically, memories of his favorite grocery store, Karol's. Wallace fondly recalls that as soon as a customer entered, "dinner cooking in the rear living quarters, and the aroma, made the visit something to look forward to." He remembers Karol's Grocery as an old-fashioned grocery store even in the 1940s. Even many years later, Wallace could recall the powerful impact the experiences the store had on his senses and memory: "Another tinkle of the bell and the slamming of the screen door meant another customer to serve. My usual purchase of a Faygo cream soda was a real treat to this little boy. My nickel or dime spent here always earned me a smile and a thank you from the man or his wife, always to be remembered to this day. A little touch of 'Mayberry' in Lincoln Park long ago." Wallace closes his memory of Karol's by calling the business a Lincoln Park institution operated by a "proud man who could always be recognized walking down Fort Street, dressed in his finest suit, white shoes and straw hat, always with his trademark of a long cigarette holder, and always a wave." Karol's Grocery closed in 1972.

JUICY FRUIT
fascinating
LUCKY STRIKE
"IT'S TOASTED"
CAROLE LOMBARD
A Winner in Any Class
10¢
SPECIAL
Nice Gifts
CORN FLAKES
Excel Seeds

Karol's Grocery Store was located at 2205 Fort Street and 2215 Fort Street. The store carried a wide variety of items including groceries, meat and ice cream. *Lincoln Park Historical Museum.*

Pictured is Karol's Grocery Store at its second location in Lincoln Park. The owners, Michael and Edna Karol, gained a reputation for quality products and top-notch customer service. *Lincoln Park Historical Museum.*

It could be said that the United States was built by those who knew how to work with lumber. The importance of wood in building anything cannot be overstated. In the Lincoln Park area, one of the most successful lumber companies was Renier. Born to parents who came to the United States from Belgium, Joseph Renier and his brother took over the lumber company founded by their father in 1924 in Detroit. The brothers went on to develop a Lincoln Park location at 1782 Howard in 1926, which grew to become one of the largest lumber supply firms in the area. In 1964, the retail store was moved a short distance south to make room for the I-75 Freeway. The business was sold to an employee, Cliff LaMora, in 1969, and it continued to operate until 1981. Joseph continued to be active in local activities until his death in 2002.

Any discussion of what a community absolutely must have in order to be considered civilized must start with discussion of a sweet shop. Mary Pacione knew about dipping chocolates long before she arrived in Detroit from Calumet in 1918. In 1925, Mary and her husband, Pasquale, a Ford Motor Company employee, moved to Lincoln Park with their daughter.

Pictured here in 1948, the Renier Company opened a lumber business on Southfield Road at Howard Street in 1926. *Lincoln Park Historical Museum.*

By the 1960s, the Renier Company had grown into a complex of twelve buildings. The business offered a wide variety of building and home improvement supplies. *Lincoln Park Historical Museum.*

Mary decided that Lincoln Park needed a business that sold sweets, and before long, the Lincoln Park Sweet Shoppe was born near the Park Theater on Fort Street. In 1939, her candy store and soda fountain expanded with the addition of a diner, and the business moved across the street to 1570 Fort Street. The shop survived the Depression and operated for over sixty-five years. Mary was an active member of the community, and she started and managed a business in a time when it was not common for women to do so. The store closed in 1991. The building is still standing and today houses an addiction treatment center.

By the 1930s, Lincoln Park—and specifically Fort Street—was developing into quite a shopping district. At the corner of Fort and Arlington Streets stood the Toleikis Building, which had a Rexall Drug Store on the first floor and apartments above. As one moved down the street, there was a Sims Men's Wear. Sims was established in Ecorse in 1923 and sold clothing for both men and boys. Lincoln Park had two Sims locations in Lincoln Park, Fort Street and the Lincoln Park Shopping Center. The original store closed in 1955, but at one time, the Sims name was well known in the Downriver area, with seven stores bearing the name. Next to Sims was the R.H. Nass Hardware Store, a shoe store and Kroger Groceries and Meats.

Continuing down Fort Street on the other side of Rexall Drugs provides a picture of a bygone era and a practice that used to be commonplace. In 1886, the Edison Illuminating Company of Detroit was founded, and the company split responsibility for providing electric power to the growing city of Detroit with Peninsular Electric Company. In 1903, the two entities merged and formed the Detroit Electric Company. By the 1930s, the Detroit Edison Company had expanded its service area to include Lincoln Park. Storefronts were set up in almost every town in Edison's service area. Each location had a manager who was active in local community affairs. Any device that ran on electricity would be fixed by service technicians for free. They also had a lightbulb exchange program. Show up at one of the retail outlets like the one on Fort Street with five burned-out lightbulbs, and the customer would be given five brand-new ones without charge. The storefronts were closed in the 1970s.

Another long-running business that was established in those early days of the city was a flower shop that has been known by more than one name and operated at several locations. In 1929, Clinton Knoch purchased a flower shop from Arthur Neiman. The original shop was located at 1415 Fort Street. As the business grew, there was a need for more room, so Knoch moved the operation to 1731 Fort Street and then later to 1429 Fort Street.

Right: This business began operations in 1925 next to the Park Theater. Early on, hand-dipped chocolates, penny candy and other sweets were available. In time, the shop expanded its offerings. Operations moved to 1570 Fort Street in 1939. Here, the storefront is shown in 1987. *Lincoln Park Historical Museum.*

Below: Just how much Lincoln Park had grown in a decade is evident from this image taken of Fort Street in the 1930s. *Lincoln Park Historical Museum.*

Looking down Fort Street from Arlington Street, one can see a wide variety of goods and services were available in this stretch. *Lincoln Park Historical Museum.*

A permanent location was acquired on the west side of Fort Street. In 1936, a greenhouse was constructed, and in later years, a garage and showrooms were added.

Ed Lobb, Clinton's son-in-law, took over managing the operation in 1954, and in 1959, he purchased the business. The shop then became known as Flowers by Lobb. Flowers have been part of the family bloodstream for almost two centuries. Ed's great-grandfather Gus Knoch was a florist in Detroit, and Gus Knoch's parents were horticulturalists in the 1800s in the Woodmere Cemetery area. Through all of the changes, the shop has thrived, and the employees and customers believe the reason is because the shop has lived up to its slogan: "Nothing is old-fashioned but our service." The shop still operates at 1382 Fort Street and guarantees all flowers will be fresh. They also sell every flower available on the market. And, of course, with time comes changes. Back when it first opened in 1929, the shop sold only fresh flowers, but now it has expanded its offerings to silk flowers, dish gardens, terrariums, fruit baskets, stuffed animals, imported lace, gift balloons and chocolates. Now going on one hundred years of operation, this business is a true Lincoln Park institution.

Over time, Fort Street became a busy thoroughfare that offered area residents a wide variety of products and services. The offerings became so plentiful and included such a variety that it could be said that if a shopper could not find what they needed along this corridor, then it might not be

Clinton Knoch established a flower shop in 1929 when he bought out Nieman's Flowers at 1415 Fort Street. The son of florists, Knoch moved his shop to 1382 Fort Street in 1936. *Lincoln Park Historical Museum.*

When Clinton Knoch retired from the floral business in the mid-1950s, he sold the operation to his son-in-law, Ed Lobb. Lobb changed the name of the business to Flowers by Lobb, and its doors continue to be open to customers to this day. *Lincoln Park Historical Museum.*

Awrey Bakeries setup a storefront at two locations in Lincoln Park: Lincoln Park Shopping Center and the store shown here on Fort Street. *Lincoln Park Historical Museum.*

available anywhere. Within walking distance was everything from groceries to clothing to hardware to dinner and desert options. Mom-and-pop businesses sat next to early chain establishments. Locally established and grown Awrey Bakeries had a storefront on Fort Street and at the Lincoln Park Shopping Center.

Awrey Bakeries got its start in 1910 in the home of Fletcher and Elizabeth Awrey, who were living in Detroit, Michigan, after moving there from Canada. To help make ends meet, Elizabeth Awrey began to bake bread and pastries in her wood-fired oven and selling products to their neighbors. When sons Wilbur, Elton and Thomas began to help sell the baked goods door to door, the business started to grow. In 1914, Awrey's opened a retail outlet on Tireman Avenue in Detroit, where the firm's first "volume baking" began. As sales increased, many additional storefronts were established. By 1950, the company had 120 locations, including both individual stores and supermarket concessions, and they also operated a home delivery service. The business operated into the twenty-first century but experienced financial difficulties due to competition. Awrey Bakeries filed for bankruptcy protection in February 2005. Five years later, Awrey was purchased and ceased to be as a brand. The business stopped operating completely in 2023.

While the twenty-first century has been inundated and now dominated with chain businesses, whether retail or food related, the backbone of the early twentieth-century community were mom-and-pop, locally grown establishments. This fact is well illustrated by a strip mall building that still stands at the southeast corner of Fort Street and Southfield Road. Through the years, tenants in this building have included Staley's Barber Shop and Lincoln (Lucas) Bar & Restaurant. Other businesses that have occupied the building include a hair salon and Central Work Clothes. Today, the structure is still standing and is occupied by AJAXX Restoration, Monster Ink Tattoo and Motorcity Graphix & Signs, with apartments on the second floor.

Lincoln Park has been home to major five-and-dime establishments throughout its history, including Woolworth's, Kresge's and Neisner Five and Dime. Brothers Abraham and Joseph Neisner opened their first variety store in Rochester, New York, in 1911. They incorporated the company in 1916, by which time they had five stores, selling merchandise from five cents to one dollar. The company prospered during the Depression, and by 1935, Neisner's had 103 stores in sixty-three cities in sixteen states.

The Lincoln Park Neisner Five and Dime location was built in 1937 with an Art Deco facade at 1716 Fort Street. The store had stainless steel panels

The intersection of Fort Street and Southfield Road has been a hub for many businesses through the years. This 1941 image shows a mini strip mall on the southeast corner. *Lincoln Park Historical Museum.*

below the windows, along with a stainless-steel trim with triangular cutouts. Above the windows were porcelain enamel panels, very typical of the era, along with a long sign that ran the width of the building. The sign had Art Deco details at each end and was the typical dime store red. According to Donald W. Wallace, who grew up in Lincoln Park in the 1930s and 1940s and wrote about his experiences in *Growing Up in Simpler Times*, Neisner's was his favorite store:

> *I remember passing the free weight scale on the sidewalk in front and my mother always giving me a coin to be put in the cloth cap of the poor man without legs selling pencils for a living in front of Neisner's....Mom would let me walk away from her so I could run to the large toy counter, overflowing with cars, trucks and everything a little boy would dream of. My gaze was on a beautiful Hopalong Cassidy Cap Gun and Holster set hanging overhead, my mother took out her small change purse after watching me gaze at this wonderful gun set. No need to put it in a bag, I strapped on this two-gun set at the counter, my mother knowing I could not have wanted anything more than this. Strutting out of Neisner Five and Dime, now with the real Hopalong Cassady Holster with two guns strapped around me, I walked down the sidewalk hoping I would be seen by other kids, but don't know if anyone noticed."*

Neisner's went bankrupt in 1977.

The building was torn down in 2015, and a Sav-A-Lot Grocery store was built on the site. The developer paid for five buildings on the block, and the company allowed the Lincoln Park Preservation Alliance to save five pieces from the facade and the sign from the back of the historic building before it was razed.

Old-world trades and skills are not given much thought in today's fast-paced machine and assembly line society. However, there was a time when these skills were much more out in front of the public view. Gus Pelton owned the Lincoln Park Tin Shop at 1706 Victoria Avenue, which provided area businesses and residents with their tin needs.

Every community needs someone or some organization whose responsibility is to chronicle the events that occur throughout its lifespan. For years, the Mellus Newspapers did just that for the city of Lincoln Park. Initially, when Lincoln Park was incorporated as a village in 1921, events were recorded by a small, eight-page weekly known as the *Lincoln Park News*. The newspaper was owned by Edward B. Gibbons. Serving as a reporting

As the construction trades thrived in the Lincoln Park area in the early 1900s, there was a call for more than just lumber. Gus Pelton owned and operated the Lincoln Park Tin Shop, which satisfied customers' needs for items made from tin. *Lincoln Park Historical Museum.*

and advertising salesman on the staff of that first endeavor was William S. Mellus. Mellus's task was to cover the events of those early days, and that included one issue that he and all residents had a very difficult time coping with: the mass of impassable mud every spring that made getting around Lincoln Park almost impossible at times. He took on the issue and became one of the most vocal advocates for better roads in the area.

Early on, Mellus decided he was going to be more than a reporter. Twice, he spearheaded a battle to keep Lincoln Park from being annexed by Detroit. In 1933, in the middle of the Depression, he started his own newspaper. His publications were praised for their well-written articles. In 1941, Mellus purchased the *Lincoln Park News*. One of his first moves was to shift from just a weekly format and publish an edition on Thursday as well. In 1942, desiring to have his own building, Mellus had a structure built at 1661 Fort Street to house his publication activities. The building was constructed in an Art Deco style called Modern. In October 1969, Panax Corporation, a chain of weekly and daily publications, acquired the *Mellus Newspaper*. Mellus stayed on as editorial and business advisor. He became interested in Lincoln Park history, and he formed the Lincoln Park Historical Commission. He also assisted in planning the Golden Jubilee celebration of Lincoln Park becoming a city.

The Mellus Newspapers were started by William Mellus in 1933. In 1942, desiring to have his own building, Mellus had a structure built at 1661 Fort Street to house his publication activities. *Lincoln Park Historical Museum.*

The *Mellus* merged with the Wyandotte-based *News-Herald* in 1985. The next year, the newspaper moved out of the Fort Street location and operated out of the *News-Herald* office in Wyandotte until moving in 1988 to One Heritage Place in Southgate. The abandoned Mellus building was placed on the National Register of Historic Places due to its important history and modern style. The front of the building contained a visual richness and character with porcelain enamel tiles, casement windows and curved glass block that went in toward the entranceway. The building remained unoccupied for over two decades. In 2010, the Mellus building was demolished.

Norton Pharmacy was located at 1660 Fort Street. It was established by Frank Norton. The year the business began is unclear, but there is a listing in the 1929 City of Lincoln Park Directory. The business grew into a popular location for the medicinal needs of the area, and at one time, it was one of the highest-volume pharmacies in the entire Downriver area. It was common to see four pharmacists working on the same shift while several clerks assisted. Robert Eldredge, who graduated from Lincoln Park High School, owned and operated the pharmacy for many years. The business was acquired by

Norton Pharmacy was started by Frank Norton. It was located at 1660 Fort Street. At one time, it was one of the highest-volume pharmacies in the Downriver area. *Lincoln Park Historical Museum.*

Arbor Drugs in the 1990s. CVS purchased Arbor Drugs in 1998, creating the largest drug retail chain in the country. While most of the former Arbor Drug locations were converted to CVS stores, some of the locations were shuttered, including the Lincoln Park location. The site became the home of the Fort Street Brewery in 2005, and that operation remained in business until 2018. The building is now for sale.

Every newly incorporated village or city needs a post office. Beginning in 1921, the year Lincoln Park was incorporated as a village, efforts were underway to acquire a branch post office of the Detroit Post Office. It took several years before a storefront location was opened in a rented building at 1471 Fort Street to accommodate the increasing population of the fast-growing village. Prior to this, mail was delivered out of the Wyandotte Post Office (for south village residents) or the Dearborn Post Office (for north residents).

In the 1930s, during the Great Depression, when the government was putting people back to work in public works programs, a more serious effort was initiated to build a new post office for the city. The U.S. Treasury approved acquisition of property that had been owned by the Quandt and Goodell families for generations at the crossroads of State Street (Southfield Road) and Fort Park Boulevard. The undeveloped lot, unofficially named Quandt Park, had been used for decades as a gathering place and sports field where baseball and horseshoes were played. Herman and Mary O. (Goodell) Quandt sold the property in January 1938 to the Treasury Department for $15,000. Plans for the construction of a building continued, with the city preferring to remain as a branch of the Detroit Post Office in order to retain advantages of the larger facilities of the Detroit office and to stay within the two-cent letter zone. Louis A. Simon, who served as supervising architect for the Public Works Branch of the Treasury, was the architect of the post office building. He served in the same capacity for a majority of similar structures built across the country in the 1930s.

Construction began in December 1938, and the new $80,000 post office was officially dedicated in a public ceremony on Friday, August 4, 1939, preceded by a parade along Fort Street from the old branch post office to the new building that attracted thousands of local residents. A dedication banquet was held at 7:00 p.m. that evening at Calvary Lutheran Church. Three days later, on Monday, August 7, the post office opened its doors to the public. James V. Southers was postal superintendent at the time. Stone carvings were cut over the front entrance and the two front windows. Each carving depicts three unique modes of mail transportation: plane, train and ship. The lobby of the building housed a mural titled *Hauling in the Nets* by Michigan artist Zoltan Sepeshy. The mural was removed and now hangs in the Marine Museum on Beaver Island, Michigan.

In the fall of 1991, the Lincoln Park Post Office moved to its current quarters at 1515 Fort Street, near the site of the original 1920s store front. In 2004, the Lincoln Park Post Office building, now 65 years old and the home of the Lincoln Park Historical Museum, was placed on the National Register of Historic Sites through the efforts of the Lincoln Park Preservation

This building used to serve as the Lincoln Park Post Office. It was built in 1939. Thousands of local residents attended a formal dedication and parade to celebrate the opening. Today, the building houses the Lincoln Park Historical Museum. *Lincoln Park Historical Museum.*

Alliance. The Post Office building was placed on the State of Michigan's Historical Sites Register in 2007.

Johnny's Nursery is another business name well known to area residents. John A. Perrella was one of two founding partners. Initially, in 1953 and for the first few years, it was a seasonal business selling flowers and produce. The business expanded to include green goods such as houseplants, evergreens and shrubs. Perrella was insistent on offering only high quality-products, and he or family members would comb a large area of the Midwest and Canada to find items suitable for Johnny's customers. After thirty years of operation, the location no longer offered perishable items and added lawn and garden supplies and landscaping tools to the store shelves. As customer interests changed over the years, Johnny's sought to cater to their wants and added home décor, garden accents, pond supplies and patio furniture. In its most successful years, Johnny's employed nine full-time people and up to forty seasonal employees. Those who worked for the Perrella family recall a warm and inviting place to work and a place that became a second home. Located at 810 Dix Avenue, Johnny's Nursery closed in 2000, and the building was torn down.

Morris Sager was a photographer who documented the evolution of the city of Lincoln Park through hundreds of images that he captured over the years. In 1937, he set up a photographic studio in a building at 2205 Fort Street. His business continued to be located in this building until 1943. Leaving this studio did not mean that Sager stopped being a photographer; he continued to document the life and times of Lincoln Park. As mentioned earlier, this building has been home to numerous businesses and today houses La Pinata Dulceria, a traditional Mexican candy store.

One of the first banks in Lincoln Park was constructed at 1605 Fort Street in 1923. It serviced area residents for decades as a bank but under many different names: Lincoln Park National Bank, State Savings Bank of Lincoln Park, Ecorse Lincoln Park Bank, Security National Bank and, finally, National City Bank. The Neoclassical design by the architectural firm Maul and Lentz was a common motif for banks in the early 1900s. The structure was built with Indiana limestone, and there was an addition built onto the original building in 1947. National City Bank was acquired by PNC Bank in 2009, and the branch at Fort Street and O'Connor was

Beginning in 1953, Johnny Parella set up a seasonal business selling flowers and produce. Over the years, the business expanded into a wide variety of garden and lawn supplies and even home décor. Johnny's Nursery was located at 810 Dix Avenue. *Lincoln Park Historical Museum.*

closed. Today, the building houses Community Care Services Turning Point Clubhouse, which is a voluntary psycho-social rehabilitation program that provides its members with a safe and inspiring environment to expand their social network, explore interests and develop new skills.

The Frank Winfield Woolworth Company (often referred to as Woolworth's) was a retail company and one of the pioneers of the five-and-dime store. It was among the most successful American and international five-and-dime businesses, setting trends and creating the modern retail model that many stores follow today. The first Woolworth store was opened in Utica, New York, on February 22, 1879, as Woolworth's Great Five Cent Store. Woolworth, along with his brother, pioneered and developed merchandising, direct purchasing, sales and customer service practices commonly used today. The original meaning of "five-and-dime store"

Top: Morris Sager documented the evolution of the city of Lincoln Park through his photography. He set up a photography studio in this building at 2205 Fort Street in 1937. *Lincoln Park Historical Museum.*

Bottom: One of the first banks in Lincoln Park, this structure was built in 1923 and originally known as the Lincoln Park National Bank. The bank changed names several times over the years, and in 1947, an addition was constructed. *Lincoln Park Historical Museum.*

Dime stores were thriving in the early 1900s. One of the most popular in Lincoln Park was the F.W. Woolworth store at 1770 Fort Street. Built in 1930, the structure still exists and now houses a Get Well Urgent Care. *Lincoln Park Historical Museum.*

referred to an establishment that sold discounted general merchandise at fixed prices, usually five or ten cents, undercutting the prices of other local merchants. Woolworth's was one of the first American retailers to put merchandise out for the shopping public to handle and select without the assistance of a salesclerk. Earlier retailers had kept all merchandise behind a counter, and customers would present the clerk with a list of items they wished to buy.

As Woolworth stores expanded across the United States, the chain invariably made its way to Michigan. The first one in Detroit was established in 1917 at the corner of Woodward Avenue and Clifford Street. A location was established in Lincoln Park in a Spanish Mission Revival–style building at 1770 Fort Street that was constructed in 1930. In the mid-1900s, the chain incorporated lunch counters, and for a time, it became the largest food-service retailer in the United States. Donald Wallace, in his book *Growing Up in Simpler Times*, relates his recollection of shopping days in Lincoln Park with his mother:

> *Woolworths was always the first stop, walking inside on the old wooden floors that creaked at times, the wonderful smell…the sales ladies all wearing colorful aprons and many with their pencil tucked into their hair bun. Mom*

always bought new thread for sewing, as I stood on my tip toes gazing at the many sales counters that were mostly filled with things I had never seen before. I recall that the sidewalks would be busy with people walking with filled shopping bags. The newspaper man on the corner of Fort Street and Southfield Road would have his papers stacked high, waiting for the cars that would line in front of Woolworths for the weekend paper to be carried to their car window. Almost all of the stores had the old type crank out sun awnings in front, while the hand crank was always left in place for the rollup at the end of the day.

Despite Woolworth's growing to be one of the largest retail chains in the world through most of the twentieth century, increased competition and a decision to focus primarily on sporting goods in the 1980s led to the store's decline. The chain went out of business in 1997. The Lincoln Park location, after closing, housed an insurance company and today is the site of a Get Well Urgent Care.

Anyone in search of legal services needed to look no further than long-term Lincoln Park attorney Frank Mixter. Born in Fairgrove, Michigan, in 1899, Mixter graduated from the Detroit College of Law in 1924 and began his Lincoln Park practice immediately. Mixter was more than just an attorney; he deeply believed in giving back to the community. He served as the board of education's attorney from 1925 until 1933 and from 1952 until his retirement in 1965. When not operating as a lawyer on behalf of the board, he served as one of the members. He donated the land on which the school system's administrative offices were built. Seven school grounds received trees donated by Mixter for the purpose of landscaping and beautification. In recognition of his contributions, the school on Electric Avenue between Pagel and Merril was named the Frank G. Mixter Elementary School.

In terms of city affairs, Mixter served as city attorney for Lincoln Park from 1929 until 1933. He was a member of the city's first library commission and served on the 1962 charter commission. Mixter spent many years as a member of the Lincoln Park Exchange Club, served as president of the organization and was instrumental in helping the group own its headquarters. During the Depression, he created a loan fund for students hoping to pursue college after graduating from high school. The Mixter Medal was first created in 1928 and was awarded on the basis of academic and athletic accomplishments. That tradition continues today at Lincoln Park High School. Frank Mixter passed away in 1983. The building at 1100 Southfield Road served as his law offices for many years. When the

This building, located at 1100 Southfield Road, served as the law offices for Lincoln Park attorney Frank Mixter. He was very involved in local affairs and organizations. *Lincoln Park Historical Museum.*

law office closed, the structure housed a State Farm agency, and today, it serves as the headquarters for Crisis Restoration and Cleaning, a recovery service for emergency building situations.

In the early 1900s, hardware stores played a pivotal role in communities as neighborhoods grew and there was a great need for construction materials, paint and tools. Halligan's Hardware Store was founded in 1923 by William J. Halligan. At the time of its founding, Fort Street was a narrow, two-lane road, and the original location was on the west side of the thoroughfare. When Fort Street was widened, Halligan's moved to the east side of the street at Fort and Cicotte Streets. Then, in 1965, an urban renewal program made one more move necessary, and the hardware store was established finally at 1586 Fort Street. In time, William's three sons, Percy, Leroy and Harold, joined their father to help manage the business, and eventually the sons became the owners and operators. The operation closed in 1976. Presently, the building is vacant.

A decent pair of shoes is essential when it comes to living a quality life. Shoe stores grew in popularity as the public demanded a wider variety of styles and types. The G.R. Kinney Company was founded in 1894 in Wavery, New York, by George Romanta Kinney. His risk became a successful venture as he sold affordably priced shoes to working Americans. By 1929, there

Halligan's Hardware Store was founded in 1923 by William J. Halligan. Over the years, the business moved three times but never very far from that original site. The last location was at 1586 Fort Street. *Lincoln Park Historical Museum.*

were 362 Kinney Shoe Stores across the United States, and the company was the largest shoe retailer. Kinney established a Lincoln Park location in 1954 on Fort Street. In 1963, the G.R. Kinney Company was sold to F.W. Woolworth. As Woolworth's struggled to compete in the late 1900s, it was announced in 1998 that all 467 Kinney Shoe Stores would close. There was a Kinney Shoe Store in two locations in Lincoln Park: 1764 Fort Street and the Lincoln Park Shopping Center.

The first bicycle shop in Lincoln Park was founded by Al and Joyce Petri in 1946. The first location, at 2176 Fort Street, was originally called Al's Bike & Toy Shop and then renamed Al Petri & Sons Bicycles. The business then moved down the street to 2160 Fort Street. A second store opened in Trenton in 1967, and another location was added in 1978 in Woodhaven. The owners always considered their venture to be the family bike shop for the community. The fourth and fifth generations of the Petri family are now actively engaged in helping provide customers' cycling needs via quality products and expert service. Petri's reputation has always stood for their friendly staff, quality brand-name bikes and expert repair services. Many current customers' parents and grandparents purchased their first bicycle from Petri's, and they now make it a family tradition to return with the next generation.

By 1929, Kinney was a national brand and the largest shoe retailer in the United States. Kinney established a Lincoln Park location on Fort Street around 1940 and the one pictured here in 1954 at the Lincoln Park Shopping Center. *Lincoln Park Historical Museum.*

In 2019, the operation consolidated into the Woodhaven location. The founder's grandson Al Petri III made the difficult decision to leave Lincoln Park. Petri's operated in Lincoln Park for over seven decades. The Petri family became known for their generosity in the community, not only serving the area's cycling needs but also participating in Lincoln Park Days,

Top: The first bicycle shop in Lincoln Park was founded by Al and Joyce Petri in 1946. The first location was at 2176 Fort Street. The business then moved down the street to 2160 Fort Street. *Lincoln Park Historical Museum.*

Bottom: Al Petri & Sons moved a short distance to this location at 2160 Fort Street. The business operated in Lincoln Park for over seven decades. After consolidating, this location closed in 2019. *Lincoln Park Historical Museum.*

partnering with safe riding programs for kids and helping with Fantasyland. The move was made because operating multiple stores was no longer fiscally viable. The building is now occupied by PEAC, which empowers individuals with disabilities through cycling, active transportation and self-advocacy education.

In 1947, Harry Weingarden started Empire Furniture in southwest Detroit. He moved the store to 2106 Fort Street in Lincoln Park in 1960. For more than fifty years, the fourteen-thousand-square-foot store offered full-service home and office furniture selection. For customers seeking accessories, no problem—the Weingarden family were always passionate about catering to the furniture needs of the Downriver community. Harry's two sons, Sid and Terry, joined the family business in the 1970s. They became well known for quality and customer service through the years, and many customers that were second and third generation would return for their furniture needs. A large warehouse behind the store meant that stock issues were lessened. At one time, the business offered six hundred fabrics and leathers to choose from. There was one unique aspect of the business: the owners decided not to operate the business with commissioned salespeople. The owners were always present to greet and help customers. The business closed in the second decade of the 2000s, and the building is now occupied by Fort Jewelry and Loan Pawn Shop.

The 1950s was a very interesting growth period for the city of Lincoln Park. It could be said that by the time the decade was over, Lincoln Park had evolved into a central location of the modern shopping age. It all began with the construction of the first major shopping center south of Detroit. Ground was broken for the Lincoln Park Plaza shopping center in 1954, centered on Fort Street and Emmons.

The twenty-two-acre site used to build the Lincoln Park Plaza has a long and interesting ownership history that dates back to the year 1750. It was in 1750 that the land on which the shopping center would be built was turned over to Antoine Robert by the Marquis de la Jonquiere, governor and lieutenant general of New France, as a grant from the French crown. The deed stated that the king of France retained all mineral rights as well as the wood found on the land. When the British gained control of the Great Lakes region after the French and Indian War, Robert's grant was considered null and void. At that point, Pierre St. Cosme persuaded the Potawatomi tribe to grant him a large tract of land that included the future site of the Lincoln Park Plaza, most of present-day Ecorse, Lincoln Park, Allen Park and part of Wyandotte. When St. Cosme died in 1787, his widow sold his landholdings.

The land passed through several owners, and in 1857, the property was purchased by Halmer H. Emmons. Emmons would later become a federal judge, and his name is now recognized as the boulevard that bisects the plaza and runs through Lincoln Park. The land passed from Emmons and eventually ended up in the hands of the developers of the plaza, land that once served as hunting ground for the Potawatomi and was laid claim to by the French and English Crowns.

The shopping center opened its doors in 1955. Initially, a major co-anchor tenant at this facility was the People's Outfitters. That endeavor did not last long, but the plaza gained a suitable replacement in Detroit-based J.L. Hudson. Starting in 1959, the well-known retailer was the headliner at the mall for the next eleven years, boasting three levels of merchandise (including a full basement). Hudson's closed the location in 1970, moving to the new Southland Mall in Taylor. The location then became best known for the grocery store Farmer Jack from the early 1970s until the early 2000s (although the basement and second floor were off limits for the remainder of its lifetime).

A listing of the original tenants of the Lincoln Park Plaza demonstrates the wide variety this shopping center offered those who ventured there: JCPenney, Kresge, People's Outfitters, Alan Lori Carpet Stores, American Health Studios, Colarossi Pizzeria, DeLore Hair Fashions, Good Housekeeping Shops, Kinsel's Drugs, Krupa's Supermarket, Leib Brothers Men's Apparel, Lerner Shops, Lincoln Park Plaza Barber Shop, Martin Oil Company, Mary Jane Shoes, Sanders, Shifrin-Willens Jewelers, Sibley's Shoes, Vanity Fair, Winkleman's and Wrigley's. In later years, competition in all of its forms eroded the profitability of many of these stores.

As of 2018, the mall was purchased by an outside firm and began preliminary restoration efforts. However, the firm has differed with what the city requires to bring structures up to code. Only 20 percent occupied, it is currently anchored by Great Lakes ACE Hardware and Dollar Tree. While most of the structures remain standing, they certainly symbolize what many consider to be the golden age of shopping.

Around the same time the Lincoln Park Plaza was being constructed, another major shopping project was being developed: the Lincoln Park Shopping Center on the corner of Dix Avenue and Southfield Road. The Lincoln Park Shopping Center is one site that will live on for years in the minds and hearts of those who shopped there. The history of the Dix Avenue and Southfield Road corner is probably one that even many locals are unaware of. In 1954, thirty acres of that site was put up for sale by

The Lincoln Park Plaza, centered on Fort Street and Emmons, opened in 1955. At one time, the shopping area had a headliner in J.L. Hudson and a wide variety of retail. *Lincoln Park Historical Museum.*

the City of Lincoln Park. Some very big names in retail were interested in the property, including J.L. Hudson, Federal's Department Stores and Sears and Roebuck. Because of the circumstances of having more than one interested party, the city council decided to auction off the property, and Sears won the auction with a bid of $450,000. The plan was to build a $2 million store on the property. Construction began in June 1955, and by August 1956, the two-story, 248,000-square-foot store was open to the public. The retail outlet was an immediate success in the area with thousands flocking there to shop.

At the time, it was the largest Sears store in the nation and the largest commercial structure that had ever been built in the Downriver area. The store employed nearly one thousand. The parking lot had spaces for three thousand cars, and the Sears building was the first of a thirty-two-unit shopping center that was planned. Within two years, the entire facility was completed with a total of thirty-four shops, two more than the original plan called for. Through the years, the complex included many well-known tenants and some lesser known: Albert's, Big Boy, Cunningham Drugs, Father and Son Shoes, Five Star Draperies, Frank's Nursery, Sanders, Giant Typewriter Mart, Hartman's, Hughes & Hatcher, Kaye's Beauty Shop, Kinney Shoes,

Top: At one time, the Sears store that was built on the corner of Southfield Road and Dix Avenue was the largest in the United States. Construction started in 1955, and the doors opened in 1956. The 248,000-square-foot structure cost $2 million to build. *Lincoln Park Historical Museum.*

Bottom: The Lincoln Park Shopping Center consisted of a hub store in Sears and thirty-four connected shops. The complex included well-known retailers as well as mom-and-pop businesses. *Lincoln Park Historical Museum.*

Kowalski Sausage, Macauley's Stationery Store, Kroger; Maling Shoes, Marianne Ladies Apparel, Meros Barber Shop, Meyer Jewelers, Nobil Shoes, Radio Shack, S.S. Kresge, Sherwin-Williams Paint Company, Sibley Shoes, Sims Men's and Boys' Wear, Stuart's Ladies' Apparel, The Branch, The Willow Tree, Three Sisters and United Shirt.

The shopping center served the community and the greater area for many decades. At one point in its history, during the 1960s, the Sears store was the chain's highest-grossing location. Attempting to keep up with the wants and needs of the public was always a challenge. In the 1980s, the center added new stores based on what surveys revealed the public wanted: Dunham's Sports, Pier 1 Imports, Winkelman's, So-Fro Fabrics and Harmony House. A Star Theater was added in 1988. During the 1990s and the first decade of the 2000s, a declining customer base caused several of the businesses to either move or close. In 2005, the shopping area known as Fairlane Green opened only a mile north of the Lincoln Park Shopping Center. Many tenants moved to this new location. The declining business traffic meant that the strip mall portion was no longer viable, and all connected buildings that were part of the Lincoln Park Shopping Center were torn down in 2018. When Sears Holdings declared bankruptcy that same year, it was announced that the Lincoln Park store would be closed. Ironically, at the time, the Lincoln Park Sears store ranked among the chain's highest-grossing stores in the country. The store closed on January 6, 2019. The building, along with the water tower, was razed in the summer of 2024. It was the end of an era for the northeast corner of Southfield Road and Dix Avenue.

BIBLIOGRAPHY

Grant, Matthew G. *Pontiac: Indian General and Statesman*. Creative Education, 1974.

Lincoln Park Preservation Alliance. *Images of America: Lincoln Park*. Arcadia Publishing, 2005.

Middleton, Richard. *Pontiac's War: Its Causes, Course, and Consequence, 1763–1765*. Routledge, 2007.

Poremba, David Lee. *Detroit: A Motor City History*. Arcadia Publishing, 2001.

Wallace, Donald W. *Growing Up in Simpler Times: Memories of Lincoln Park*. Donald Walter Wallace, 2013.

INDEX

ABOUT THE AUTHOR

Craig Hutchison is a historian, author, historical interpreter and researcher. He has worked in history-related positions for such institutions as the Henry Ford Estate, The Henry Ford, Wayne County Parks and the Dearborn Historical Museum. A lifelong resident of Dearborn, Michigan, Craig earned a BA in history from the University of Michigan. The study of history, writing and having his writings published are his greatest passions. While at the Wayne County Parks, Craig served on the National Heritage Area project, helping write the history portion of a proposal that resulted in the Detroit Metropolitan area being named the MotorCities National Heritage Area. Craig has never been far from the history of Henry Ford. While at the Henry Ford Estate, he worked on projects related to the interpretation of Ford history including the improvement of tour and reenactment activities. Working as a historical interpreter at Greenfield Village, guiding the public as to what life was like in the past provided an enlightening perspective as to how the public views historical topics. The Dearborn Historical Museum opened a whole new world as Craig had the opportunity to serve as the institution's communications specialist. Presently, he is the editor of the *Dearborn Historian*, a quarterly publication of the Dearborn Historical Museum. The greatest thrill for Craig is to share historical information with the public, and he has been able to live out his dream through the publication of five history-related publications. It is his hope that *Lost Lincoln Park* will be both informative and interesting to readers while also serving to preserve the very important stories of Lincoln Park structures and the people associated with them.

Visit us at
www.historypress.com